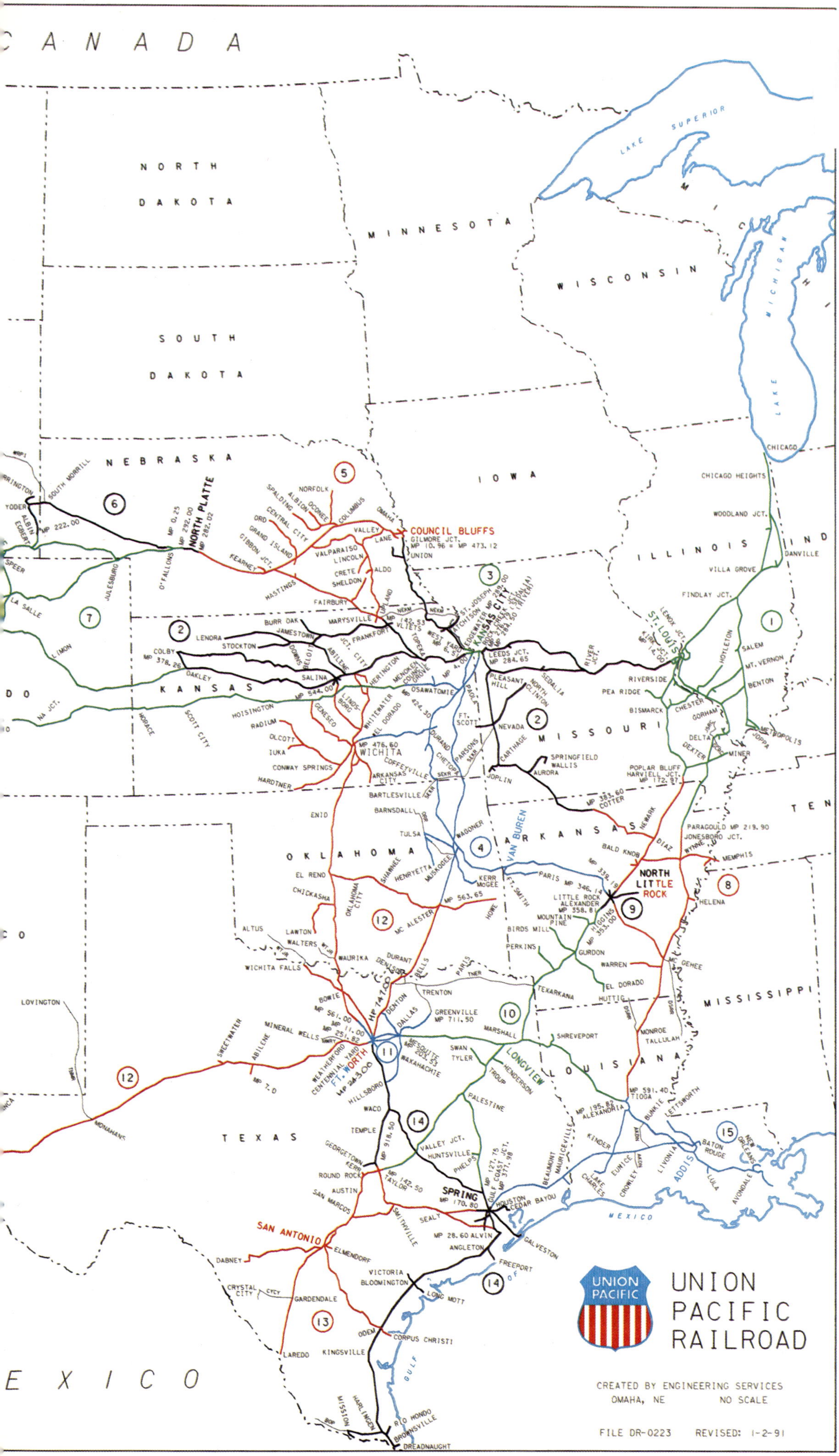
CANADA
NORTH DAKOTA
SOUTH DAKOTA
MINNESOTA
WISCONSIN
LAKE SUPERIOR
LAKE MICHIGAN
MICHIGAN
IOWA
NEBRASKA
ILLINOIS
IND
KANSAS
MISSOURI
OKLAHOMA
ARKANSAS
TEN
MISSISSIPPI
LOUISIANA
TEXAS
MEXICO
GULF OF MEXICO
CHICAGO
CHICAGO HEIGHTS
WOODLAND JCT.
DANVILLE
VILLA GROVE
FINDLAY JCT.
ST. LOUIS
SALEM
MT. VERNON
BENTON
RIVERSIDE
PEA RIDGE
BISMARCK
CHESTER
GORHAM
DELTA
DEXTER
MINER
JOPPA
METROPOLIS
POPLAR BLUFF
HARVIELL JCT.
MP 172.97
NORTH PLATTE
MP 282.02
O'FALLONS
JULESBURG
LA SALLE
LIMON
YODER
SOUTH MORRILL
MP 222.00
COUNCIL BLUFFS
GILMORE JCT.
MP 10.96 = MP 473.12
UNION
OMAHA
NORFOLK
SPALDING
ALBION
OCONEE
COLUMBUS
CENTRAL CITY
ORD
GRAND ISLAND
GIBBON
FEARNEY
VALLEY
LANE
VALPARAISO
LINCOLN
CRETE
SHELDON
ALDO
HASTINGS
FAIRBURY
MARYSVILLE
BURR OAK
JAMESTOWN
LENORA
STOCKTON
COLBY
MP 378.26
OAKLEY
SALINA
MP 544.00
ABILENE
FRANKFORT
TOPEKA
ST. JOSEPH
ATCHISON
KANSAS CITY
LEEDS JCT.
MP 284.65
PLEASANT HILL
SEDALIA
RIVER JCT.
HERINGTON
OSAWATOMIE
PAOLA
LINDSBORG
GENESEO
HOISINGTON
RADIUM
OLCOTT
IUKA
CONWAY SPRINGS
HARDTNER
SCOTT CITY
HORACE
WHITEWATER
EL DORADO
WICHITA
MP 476.60
ARKANSAS CITY
COFFEYVILLE
FT. SCOTT
NEVADA
CARTHAGE
JOPLIN
SPRINGFIELD
WALLIS
AURORA
COTTER
MP 383.60
NEWARK
DIAZ
PARAGOULD MP 219.90
JONESBORO JCT.
WYNNE
MEMPHIS
BALD KNOB
NORTH LITTLE ROCK
HELENA
BARTLESVILLE
BARNSDALL
ENID
TULSA
WAGONER
VAN BUREN
HENRYETTA
MUSKOGEE
SHAWNEE
EL RENO
CHICKASHA
OKLAHOMA CITY
KERR MCGEE
FT. SMITH
PARIS MP 346.14
LITTLE ROCK
ALEXANDER
MP 358.81
MOUNTAIN PINE
BIRDS MILL
PERKINS
GURDON
WARREN
EL DORADO
MC GEHEE
MP 563.65
MC ALESTER
HOWE
ALTUS
LAWTON
WALTERS
WICHITA FALLS
WAURIKA
DURANT
DENISON
PARIS
TRENTON
TEXARKANA
HUTTIG
MONROE
TALLULAH
SHREVEPORT
GREENVILLE
MP 711.50
MARSHALL
LONGVIEW
TYLER
HENDERSON
TROUP
PALESTINE
BOWIE
DENTON
DALLAS
FT. WORTH
MINERAL WELLS
WEATHERFORD
CENTENNIAL YARD
ABILENE
SWEETWATER
LOVINGTON
MONAHANS
MESQUITE
WAXAHACHIE
HILLSBORO
WACO
TEMPLE
GEORGETOWN
KERR
ROUND ROCK
AUSTIN
SAN MARCOS
TAYLOR
VALLEY JCT.
HUNTSVILLE
PHELPS
SPRING
MP 170.80
HOUSTON
CEDAR BAYOU
BEAUMONT
MAURICEVILLE
MP 195.82
ALEXANDRIA
KINDER
EUNICE
CROWLEY
LAKE CHARLES
LIVONIA
ADDIS
BATON ROUGE
NEW ORLEANS
LULA
AVONDALE
BUNKIE
LETTSWORTH
MP 591.40
TIOGA
SAN ANTONIO
SMITHVILLE
SEALY
MP 28.60 ALVIN
ANGLETON
GALVESTON
FREEPORT
DABNEY
ELMENDORF
VICTORIA
BLOOMINGTON
CRYSTAL CITY
GARDENDALE
LONG MOTT
ODEM
CORPUS CHRISTI
LAREDO
KINGSVILLE
MISSION
HARLINGEN
RIO HONDO
BROWNSVILLE
DREADNAUGHT
UNION PACIFIC
UNION PACIFIC RAILROAD
CREATED BY ENGINEERING SERVICES
OMAHA, NE NO SCALE
FILE DR-0223 REVISED: 1-2-91

9270
UNION PACIFIC
9343

UNION PACIFIC'S WEST

By Donald Sims

PHOTOGRAPHS BY THE AUTHOR

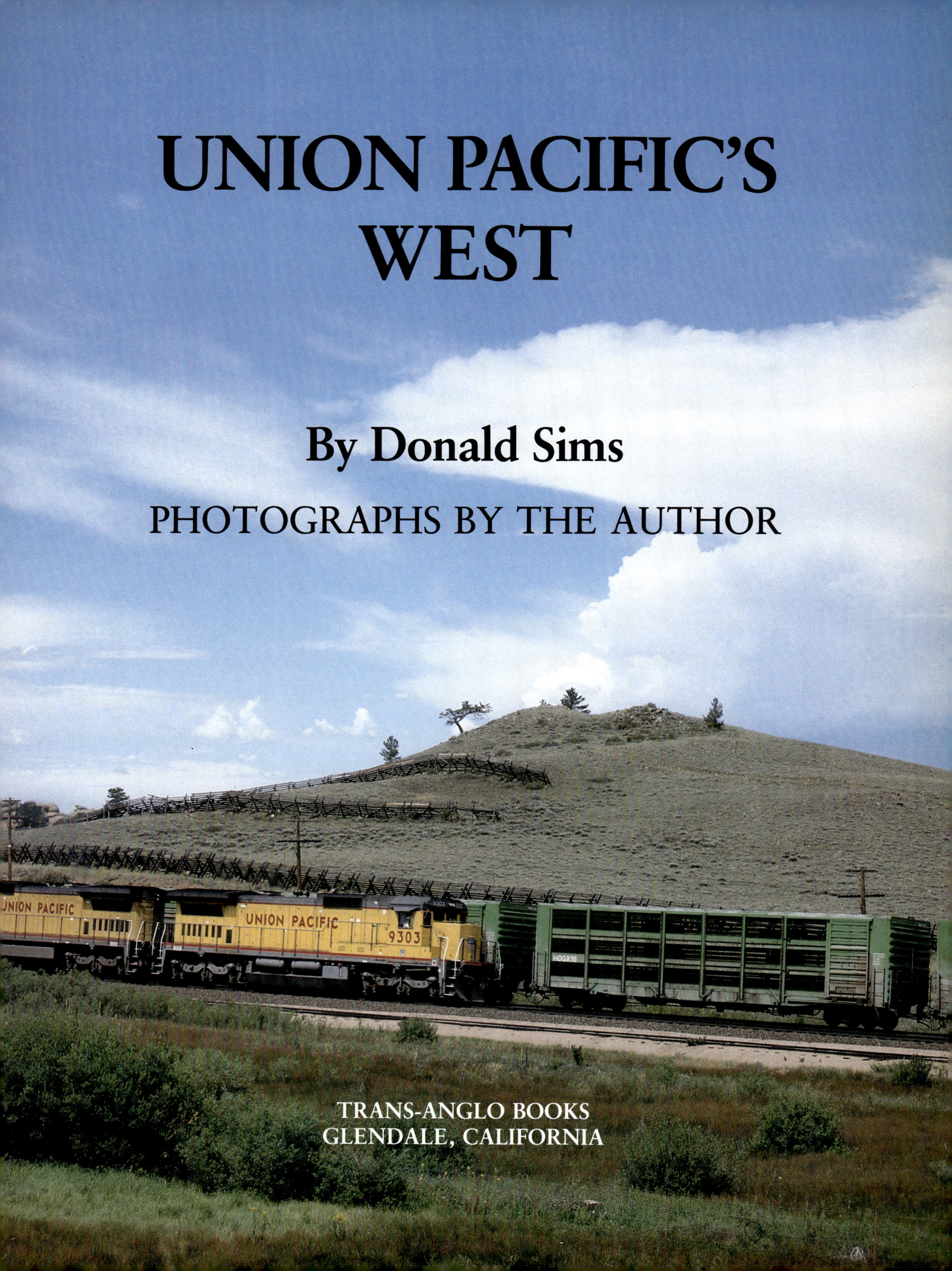

TRANS-ANGLO BOOKS
GLENDALE, CALIFORNIA

Front Dust Jacket: Sixteen thousand horsepower are needed to forward a solid cut of auto racks off the northwest docks and into the Midwest. The locale is near Motanic on the western slopes of the Blue Mountain grade.

Frontispiece: A pig train and an eastbound "Z" go their opposite way on Sherman Hill in the vicinity of Dale. If there was any doubt about the status of the piggybacker, check out the UPS trailers tagging along behind the engine.

Rear Endsheet: Following a depression along the Snake River, a container train is stretched along a gentle curve near Glenns Ferry, Idaho.

Rear Dust Jacket: Train time at Green River, Wyoming, is typically crowded. Three sets of westbound power wait for a soon-to-arrive stack train on the far left track.

UNION PACIFIC'S WEST

Manufactured in the United States of America

Edited by Bill Bradley and David Giglio

Layout and Book Design by Bill Bradley

Typesetting by Roc-Pacific

First Printing: Spring 1991

Published by
Trans-Anglo Books
A Division of INTERURBAN PRESS
P.O. Box 6444 □ Glendale, California 91225-0444

Library of Congress Cataloging-in-Publication Data

Sims, Donald.
Union Pacific's West / by Donald Sims ; photographs by the author.
p. cm.
ISBN 0-87046-098-6
1. Union Pacific Railroad Company. I. Title.
TF25.UBS58 1991
385'.0978—dc20 91-2894
CIP
AC

CONTENTS

UNION PACIFIC
UNION PACIFIC

INTRODUCTION

SIMPLY PUT, UNION PACIFIC is a name linked inseparably with railroading, one that has worn history well.

The purpose of a railroad, as anyone knows, is to run trains. Some railroads do an excellent job of that; others are characterized as average performers, while an expression of "ho hum" probably fits a few. On Union Pacific rails, "superbly" is undoubtedly the proper adjective. This railroad's longtime slogan, "We Can Handle It," is not a promotional convenience but a philosophy, an operating conscience of routine expectations.

This book concerns itself with the Union Pacific Railroad west of Omaha, not today's overall system which incorporates Missouri Pacific and the onetime Missouri-Kansas-Texas Railroad, but the original UP, plus one annexation, ex-Western Pacific steel which fits exceedingly well into that statement, "Omaha and beyond." Such is an arbitrary distinction, an advantage of self-choice as well as some logic. Acquisition of the "Wobbly" gave Omaha's management the brass ring, completing this railroad's access to the last major commercial port on the Pacific Coast it did not already serve.

Stack trains, intermodal traffic, lengthy cuts of auto racks; this is heady stuff to a traffic manager, and its roots extend down to tidewater, making UP ideally situated to cash in on that Pacific Rim/Land Bridge action which is being projected by popular acclaim.

Now we can begin to contemplate Union Pacific, a railroad of legendary historical significance and contemporary acclaim. Emphatically the latter.

Pick your day, any day! The hour is your choice, too!

Imagine what railroading's like throughout UP's West. Out there, one-third of western America is home to a clan dressed in armour yellow, the modern trademark of a perpetually restless fleet of diesel locomotives.

Focus on Fremont, Nebraska, where Chicago and Northwestern cozies up to a great steel turnpike that sprints west out of Council Bluffs on the Missouri River. Approaching its partner at an oblique angle, C&NW

Opposite: Illustrating what the Dash-8 can do for you, two units are able to handle this train crossing a tall bridge at American Falls, Idaho. In other days, a three-unit set of SD40s would probably be coupled on.

delivers and receives thousands of cars each calendar month, providing the Chicago connection for UP. Just now the LACSZ symbol, two days and almost 2,000 miles removed from Los Angeles, is slowly threading its way onto North Western iron, its home road odyssey at an end, its next-on C&NW crew standing trackside, poised, valises in hand to launch the last lap toward the Windy City's Canal Street terminus. A high-stepper, this run swings into Fremont with a flourish.

Out in Wyoming, a quartet of veteran, hard-breathing SD40s is grasping for the 8,000-foot crest of Sherman Hill, stretching 10,000 tons of westbound grain on a tenacious, if unspectacular, march toward an ocean port. Meantime, generating a steady 70-mph course to which it is accustomed at every possible opportunity, a double-stacked container symbol races through Idaho, owing its abilities to the latest example of a locomotive builder's blueprint, 4,000 hp worth of computer-controlled internal combustion energy in a single housing, and 70 feet of concentrated muscle which once came in three units, not one.

Union Pacific owns hundreds of these powerful behemoths.

In the midst of all this up-to-date, state-of-the-art commentary, an anachronism comes rumbling down the old Los Angeles and Salt Lake Railroad pathway. Tied just behind the diesel's drawbars of a westbound hotshot, a half-dozen stock cars trail along, their somewhat fragrant cargo ultimately destined for the cold cases of Southern California supermarkets. Although seemingly out of place in this final decade of the 20th century, this anachronism is quite logical in the context of UP's mindset. It's profitable.

So are sugar beets, wood chips and many other items, which, while not trendy or major contributors to the bottom line, add their modest share to the business of being a railroad.

Then there is coal. On the windswept plains of western Nebraska, a onetime almost abandoned branch now hums to a 30-train-a-day tempo. That's today; tomorrow the railroad is expecting even more.

In linear dimensions, one railroad is clearly greater than another even if their width is on a par. Of the 23,000-odd miles that represent today's combined UP-WP-MoPac-Katy system, some 10,000 represent the western scene across the Missouri River beyond Omaha.

Standardization does not mean that one carrier is just like another, no matter their equalities in gauge, motive power or rolling stock. To provide substance to this notion, we compared certain physical features of the original UP with those of MoPac mainline segments. Though hardly a scientific or statistically accurate survey, the criteria of MoPac-UP match-ups were: (a) mainline subdivisions; and (b) that they be signaled, generally of a Centralized Traffic Control (CTC) profile or, on a few occasions, Automatic Block Signal (ABS) systems.

By checking through the pages of a current systemwide timetable, we developed some interesting comparisons. Save for a limited number of very difficult terrain areas, e.g., the Feather River Canyon in California, or Oregon's Blue Mountain redoubt, Union Pacific clearly emerged overall as a faster railroad than Missouri Pacific.

The MOP recorded 20 principal subdivisions whose top freight train speed was recorded as 60 mph, while seven other segments came in at 50 mph or at 45 mph. On the other hand, Union Pacific published a 70-mph standard over most of 14 subs; four were limited to a 55–60-mph maximum and eight weighed in with a 50-mph pace or just below. Typically, these latter were contoured through more difficult landscape than what lies east of the Rocky Mountains, where MoPac is concentrated.

Where Amtrak ran, UP allowed 79 mph, Missouri Pacific 75 mph.

Since motive power wanders with equal nimbleness throughout the expansive combination, this rough analysis suggests that steel west of Omaha is slightly superior, if only by a slight degree. But this very basic comparison did not look at signal systems, stage length of crew runs or any other standard, so draw your own conclusions. Still, as the final decade of the century dawns, it appears one-half bests the other, if only temporarily.

At first glance, today's Union Pacific Railroad presents a very impressive image. Like a beauty contest queen, it displays all the proper proportions of greatness. These include transcontinental reach, a well-groomed motive power fleet which typically includes the latest models, good connections to the rest of the nation, as well as a multitude of other contemporary dimensions by which a railroad is judged.

"We Can Handle It" underscores the first-rate performance led by a yellow flotilla through the expansiveness of western America.

Union Pacific runs on a four-foot, 8½-inch base like any other American railroad, meaning there are tens of thousands of other miles out there of equal potential. The question then is, what makes this particular company unique, different or, for that matter, individualistic? A tiny part of that answer might lie in where it sets foot, but there is a lot more to Union Pacific than geographical diversity.

The real story is how it does it, the way it does it, and the personality that results.

If you're searching for some quantifiable clue of what UP is about, you need look no further than ground level or, more precisely, the date stamps on its welded steel underpinnings. Much of its immaculately groomed main line exhibits a 1980s' rolling mill date stamp, generally of 133-pound cross-section. Confident of this quality, the railroad's multitude of time-urgent schedules can fly across the landscape at "70 per," with the reassurance that a specialized track vehicle has routinely been utilizing electronic sensors to search for flaws.

A hundred-year-old building in downtown Omaha now boasts the absolute ultimate in train control technology, spreading its mantle to the far reaches of the West Coast and just about everywhere beyond the Missouri River. "Black box" controls have been introduced to hundreds of recently arrived diesel locomotives, assuring the railroad keeps out front on the learning curve.

This and dozens of ongoing programs measure an ability to stay competitive, to confront rubber-tired 18-wheelers on their tax-supported concrete passageways. There are also those traditional foes robed in steel, Santa Fe, Espee, the Burlington Northern.

Literally from birth, since the day a path was spiked down into a form of iron and wood and motion, the important railroads—or those that aspire to that position—have been forged into a perpetual course of evolution. Change, now noted as "high-tech," is forever, not all at once but usually in fits and starts of irregular patterns. So it has been since the first tiny fireboxes led to boiler pressure and moving wheels. Few railroads are more aware of this than Union Pacific.

Today, innovation often arrives in multiples of fancy name tags. One need only admire GE's Dash-8 heavyweight or an EMD wide cab of the most recent delivery date to properly appreciate that trend line.

Hot box detectors; radio-based sensors; high, wide or dragging equipment indicators; cab signals, and centralized traffic control for the entire railroad . . . none were placed on the roadbed at a single moment, but in measured, frequently upgraded increments. Typically, Union Pacific is normally far out on the leading edge of that tide.

Merely writing a check for new equipment by itself won't resolve all the competitive issues. Honing, adjusting to new capabilities, and constant analysis are the key. Besting your rivals is not a now-and-then knee-jerk reaction but a continual process of assimilation. Such are the realities if you want to lead rather than follow in another's dust.

Thus, at any moment in Union Pacific's backyard something will be evolving: a new prime mover just delivered and being set up with a bit of customizing at North Platte's massive shop, perhaps some developmental engineers huddled over newly embedded sensors in the roadbed, seeing if perhaps this latest control technique can hustle a few precious moments from tomorrow's schedules.

Before proceeding too much further, it has become necessary to take note of a last-minute modification in Union Pacific's jurisdictional alignment, proving, of course, that little is static about this particular railroad. And while the railroad may eschew the old traditions, it has created a new one, change. This is late 20th-century conventionalism, termed *innovation.*

This book was already far along in production when it was discovered that UP had altered its divisional structure, realigning some, generating new entities in other instances. Insofar as the western half of the railroad is concerned, the restructuring includes the following, none of which has any effect whatsoever on the physical presence or descriptions, only upon management responsibilities. We apologize in advance, but we want to explain why some descriptions vary a bit from the latest system map of early 1991 which accompanies the text.

Wooden soldier-like in their uniformity, small towns line the roadbed of central Nebraska, each marked by a grain elevator. It is territory through which modern diesels run at flank speed, no matter their burden.

In one change, clearly obvious from its growing importance, the North Platte Subdivision has been elevated to the status of the "North Platte Division." The ex-Western Pacific dichotomy of Nevada and Feather River Divisions has been consolidated into a single Feather River Division, jurisdiction extending west of Salt Lake City and encompassing in its entirety, the old "Wobbly."

Wherever Seaport and Spokane Divisions are mentioned, inject the new name, Columbia River Division, which has swallowed up both. Idaho Division, a name from the recent past, has been reincarnated, replacing the Nampa and Pocatello Divisions of recent status. The Green River and Cheyenne Divisions have had their boundaries altered, in the process eliminating Wyoming Division references. In eastern Kansas and Nebraska, a newly minted Midwest Division name now substitutes for the late Wichita and Kansas Divisions.

All this proves is that it is difficult to keep up a fast-paced Union Pacific.

In conclusion, we would like to refer to the genre of cigarette company advertisements. They display two categories of imagery. One is a well-groomed, sophisticated, obviously corporate type of personality, while the other features the macho breed, cowboy, oil well driller, helicopter pilot, whatever. Well, UP's likeness embraces both categories. It is the image of success blended with the brawny, physical prowess of the other.

This railroad will not let chance control events.

If you happened to be a theatrical agent booking Union Pacific's routine into performances around the nation, you would probably describe it as a class act.

Let's discover why!

UNION PACIFIC
3442
3803

THE GREAT STEEL TURNPIKE

UNION PACIFIC'S WEST contains many prominent geographic features. The Blue Mountains in Oregon, the solitary desert south and west of Salt Lake City, the Columbia River Gorge, and the always unpredictable Feather River Canyon are but a few. Yet one of the most outstanding features of the railroad is the thousand miles of twin-tracked roadbed between Council Bluffs and Salt Lake City.

Today, this great steel turnpike, which began as UP's portion of the original transcontinental railroad, is the heart of the system. Dozens of train movements, fast running and high pressure, characterize the railroad. On this line, yesterday's traditions are not necessarily a valid response to present need.

Like the handle of a pitchfork—with three single-track routes to Pacific Coast ports serving as prongs—UP's ever-busy steel turnpike introduces Midwest plains to western mountains and basins. Humidity, thunderstorms and blinding blizzards descend on a vast empire of high-altitude and parched desert where emptiness is fact, not fiction.

From either direction, the steel assaults the 8,000-foot profile of Sherman Hill, while North Platte's twin humps tear apart and reunite dozens of daily trains through one of the land's largest retarder yards—a smooth-functioning link envied by competitors.

Until the past few years this great steel highway was part of the Nebraska and Wyoming Divisions. UP used to align operating units with the states in which they ran, but today breaks them down into somewhat smaller but more logically defined units.

Starting from its eastern tip, at Omaha–Council Bluffs, the now-foreshortened Nebraska Division, with its mostly ABS-controlled double track, extends westward across the rising plains from milepost zero to milepost 282 just short of North Platte. Here the abbreviated North Platte Service Unit appears, its strategic terminal holding the principal key to UP's entire western territory.

The westward journey beyond North Platte's terminal continues

Opposite: A farm tractor kicks up dust as a speeding train scurries by on the steel turnpike in western Nebraska.

under Cheyenne Division aegis, and from here to Salt Lake City the bulk of train control is CTC, which, along with the twin set of heavy-duty steel, gives dispatchers maximum flexibility in running their high capacity railroad.

Sherman Hill juts above the spreading plains just west of Cheyenne, an operating barrier mastered in today's world by an application of horsepower in massive measurements. While the total stage length from North Platte through Cheyenne and just past Rawlins has long been pushbutton dispatching of the electronic school of thought, almost a hundred miles of ABS running style appears at Riner, effective to near Rock Springs, Wyoming.

Terms like "twin track" or "double track" are used alternately between Salt Lake City and Omaha, providing measurable differences in the way Union Pacific functions. Twin-track running is interpreted as "either track/either direction," the most flexible tool available, while "double track" indicates solo directional moves on either set of rails—except for rules defined as "against the current of traffic," a very restrictive concept and not attuned to routine needs of densely packed train movements.

There are some sections west of Omaha where territorial/traffic considerations can be accomplished by "double track," but the bulk of mileage on the turnpike features bi-directional input out of Omaha.

The Green River Division takes over the mesa-strewn landscape of western Wyoming. Rule 251 is in command, a prescription of how trains should conduct themselves on double-track sections. Those center sidings with their equal access from either track, either end, have been a feature for a few hundred miles since Council Bluffs, and they come in handy under Rule 251, providing an outlet where hotshots can overtake their slower brethren moving the same way. The whole world's a siding with twin tracks where CTC's pulling the strings in conjunction with intermittent crossovers, but in block signal territory under double-track rules, the siding's the thing. Not all passing tracks are of the mid-course variety. Frequently they are to one side or the other but reachable from either main by virtue of switchpoints. Siding lengths typically extend to 9,000–12,000 feet, available for even the longest of trains

Named for its centerpiece division point, the Green River Division is a reflection of just how busy this railroad can be. One recent day a visitor popped into local headquarters, a large Roman-columned station at Green River, and casually inquired about the next few hours of train movements. Proffering the latest lineup, a trainmaster muttered something about it being average, 52 trains called over the next 18 hours, subject to modification, meaning that perhaps a few more would be announced as traffic developed here or there.

Opposite: Sherman Hill near Dale Junction. A deep cut leads toward tunnels as UP takes what nature will give in the conquest of this 8,000-foot-high summit.

Beyond through movements—doublestacks, the general freights, piggybackers at speed—UP generates a great deal of on-line carloadings between Omaha and Great Salt Lake. Large numbers of coal, iron ore,

3675
2950

A measure of its often busy stature, Green River has five mainline signals funneling into the main stem for eastbound movements. Note that each has an "End AC" (automatic cab signals) for trains arriving from the east. Here, a fast-paced trailer train is getting a wheel on things as it leaves for eastern points.

grain and soda ash trains are penciled in daily making this one of the busiest rail lines west of the Mississippi River.

After climbing out of Green River on a short, steep ascent, UP iron initiates the first of three breakaways to Pacific Coast ports, today's business bonanza.

At Granger, Control Point CP847—with its 40-mph turnout—diverts traffic onto a single-track line that eventually leads to yards at Pocatello, Portland, Seattle and a half dozen other northwest locations. Meantime, the long twin tracks carry fast-moving traffic on toward Mormon country. Fast-paced, yes, but not without a few hills to climb or descend, for the country west of Green River is laced with bluffs, plateaus and mesas.

Before the Wyoming–Utah state line, Altamont's rise must be scaled. Then there's a brief ripple in the landscape close to Evanston, after which a narrow descent of Weber Canyon is required along with a modicum of left-hand running—a necessity from an earlier epoch when gradient and smaller motive power could be compensated for by clever handling of cuts, fill and tunneling.

Just as Ogden is reached, East Riverdale Yard looms, the edge of a terminal area where interchange is made with Southern Pacific. Now Utah Division takes over. Although twin tracks continue after making a southern turn toward Salt Lake City, the fascinating profile of UP is almost over. The last lap of the steel turnpike is 37 miles of controlled roadbed between Ogden and Salt Lake City. From then on, the single tracks to the coast bind work to their own rules and independent geography.

This great road west of the Missouri River happens to be one of railroading's outstanding showpieces. Let's examine how Union Pacific makes it work.

Opposite: A load of welded steel rail waits for a crew at Green River, while an inbound chemical train heads into a yard seemingly full of loaded hoppers.

3371
UNION PACIFIC
3839
3287
UNION PACIFIC

9172
9172
UNION PACIFIC

Unlike many railroads where switcher corps is based upon small horsepower units, UP assigns 3,000-hp units to yards like Green River, where long cuts of chemical hauling hoppers tax even the muscle of an SD40.

Opposite: This westbound hotshot wheeling out of Green River has barely allowed crews to do more than exchange brief remarks about the diesel's performance and condition. Two, perhaps three minutes, have elapsed since the arriving crew stepped aside for a new one.

At Green River, a three-unit set begins backing up to get the second half of a westbound hopper train.

Over toward Rawlins, Wyoming, the line passes through the wide open spaces of south-central Wyoming, where an occasional hill makes an appearance. During the winter, the railroad's foe is blowing snow, which is why snow fences are a necessity.

Opposite, top: Montana bills itself as Big Sky Country, but can Wyoming be far behind? Just west of Green River's ever-busy terminal, a pair of Dash-8s takes on the grade of a long, curving hill on their way to Salt Lake City.

Opposite, below: The sun is about to disappear over a wintry horizon as a westbound freight speeds along the Utah-Wyoming border.

9169 9169
UNION PACIFIC
9169
9124 9124
9124
UNION PACIFIC

9125 9125

A cross-section of Omaha's systemwide control room illustrates one portion of the latest in dispatching technology. On the background wall are projections that can be moved from one panel to another as required.

PHOTO COURTESY OF UNION PACIFIC

AKA Railroad in a Room

By late 1990 UP will be dispatching its 700 daily trains from a building near downtown Omaha that is commonly called the "Bunker." Built in 1891, it served as a freight house until 1977, and was resurrected to become the latest in railroad command centers, equivalent to a railroad in a room.

Officially dubbed the Harriman Dispatching Center, it exists in surrealistic isolation from three-dimensional railroading. You don't hear the thunder or feel the shock of pounding trains, nor can you inhale the pungent scent of burnt diesel. Seemingly not part of the outside world it so strictly dominates, the bunker exudes the hushed, overbearing attitude of the electronic age, sort of a superiority complex which only a limited number of people are privileged to understand. There is no need to shout in its presence; indeed, the dispatchers who command its pushbutton wizardry converse in soothing tones.

At North Platte's dispatching center, as a train rolled off one CTC panel to another, the dispatcher would holler, "Got one coming atchya," a cry still heard in late 1989. But as North Platte's functions are taken over by Harriman, this sort of outgoing tradition will probably become socially taboo.

Each morning a group of managers meets in the bunker to review the past 24 hours. Like all good brass hats, they want to analyze performance, how many schedules toed the mark, how many missed and why. Yesterday that sort of statistic was available possibly a day or two past events; today's behavioral science is available instantly, or however long it takes a high-speed printer to respond. Also at hand is a complete analysis of what motive power is available and the up-to-date status of all yards.

Four geographical compartments, eastern, western, southern and central, oversee train activities. A similar alignment is set up with motive power management, rolling stock, maintenance-of-way and other activities.

As referred to elsewhere, this computerized railroad management system routinely makes motive power assignments and "what-if" scenarios about running UP's railroad efficiently, options that a human mind would be incapable of solving in the figurative wink of an eyelash. Over the 10,000 or so miles of the original UP map beyond Omaha there are approximately 1,700 control points logged into this system. A "CP" can be a signal, a signal-switch combination or a readout sensor for such events as dragging equipment, hot boxes, high/wide loads and the like.

From a smoke-tinted, glassed-in amphitheater that extends below and to either side of management's raised platform, dozens of winking lights chart the progress of three-dimensional reality across a giant, systemwide schematic. A 15-foot-high video screen extends down each wall, roughly the length of a football field. There are 32 dispatching stations available along with a quartet of spares, and when the entire operation is functioning by late 1990 it will be controlling 23,000 miles of railroad action.

Flexibility is the watchword, as the track diagram for each dispatching station is projected on a screen, and is therefore not a permanent track diagram. If required because of events, part or all of one dispatching territory can be switched over to a spare, or interchanged with a different location. The Harriman Center replaces 10 widespread regional control centers, putting the entire railroad's visual perspective into a single locale.

So as one strides up and down the building, the electronic generalship of a huge railroad system is immediately obvious, backed up by whatever statistical support can conceivably be utilized. All in real time!

You can literally, visually, see every train currently occupying a mainline position anywhere that UP roadbed sets foot. A light will confirm its presence, matching it with the name and location of every siding or control point from Omaha to Seattle, from Denver to Kansas City or from Chicago to Houston.

Yet this is just a beginning. From this foundation more and more electronic magic will be added. Already road tests have been made with embedded roadbed sensors, controls that enable a dispatcher to start and stop trains or run them untouched by human hands. If and when that prospect ever dominates mainline action, Union Pacific will be well positioned to reap the benefits.

Apparently with enough fuel aboard to bypass the service station at Rawlins, SD40 No. 3526 has stopped short of the hoses. A new crew walks across the tracks for the next lap of an eastbound trek.

The Service Station

Taming a slow curve here or there, buying heftier prime movers, moving them with computerized signals, perhaps installing a high-speed turnout at a key junction—these will help save hours between Chicago and Seattle or on any long haul. The same could be said for better locomotive utilization and servicing, which brings us to Rawlins, Wyoming.

Long shadows late on an August day profile a set of diesel fuel racks serving four tracks of mainline stature. This is one of UP's mainline fueling stands, just one more item in a laundry list of ideas created to pare handling time from Point A to Point Z. Momentarily it is empty, and perhaps will be for an hour or so, as the bunching of train action is a familiar theme here, as elsewhere on the system.

Soon, though, action is on tap, to be performed on the main while train crews exchange duties. Fuel is pumped aboard while engines stay coupled to their charges.

From the east comes a set of SD40s, including one whose armour yellow is sun-bleached to a faded, chalky hue after years of hard labor. Perhaps a candidate for rebuilding, possibly destined soon for a scrap heap in this season of SD60s and muscular Dash-8s, it has justified its investment by rolling for well over a million miles—just as every unit of mainline physique is expected to do. Towing a waybill list of boxcars, gons and flats, the older series of prime movers is hardly mated to a prima donna, just your average freight train. A quick check of fuel gauges shows they're reasonably full, so a servicing crew can let them move on untouched.

Little hurry seems evident at this point as a second westbound soon moves through the long, sweeping curve east of town, its headlight cutting an increasingly brilliant contrast in a fast-approaching twilight. Rumbling to a halt beside the earlier arrival, this latest one trails one hundred car lengths of grain mated behind another three-unit lashup of Forties, including an ex-MoPac diesel without a dynamic brake bulge. Aromas of warm grease and burnt diesel waft over fueling stanchions, creating impressions of suppressed action.

A few minutes tick by as fuel is added to the partially empty tanks of this new arrival. Meanwhile, a couple of outbound crews mill around the nearby yard office, seemingly in no hurry to depart.

There are four mainline tracks that go through this diesel service station at Rawlins, where fuel is added to many of the diesel lashups. Generally, an eastbound train's units are filled if they average less than 2,200 gallons per unit, and a westbound's if they have less than 2,800–3,300 gallons, depending on the destination.

Then a third arrival announces its presence, softly gliding to a stop as an engineer deftly allows his tonnage to work toward retarding motion. At each end of this fueling stop, sets of block signals glow brilliant red, topping "END ACS" signs reminding all that cab signal control is a vital part of this railroad.

Now three westbounds are marking time, their departure as yet a mystery. Only a single main alley remains open, still a remarkable vista for those accustomed to western-style, single-track railroading.

The last arrival's fuel tanks are also topped off, since less than 3,000 gallons of diesel energy remain. As a rough rule of thumb, eastward-bound units can go unrefueled if they have at least 2,200 gallons showing on their gauges, while the standard for westward trains fluctuates between 2,800 and 3,300 gallons, depending on just where they are headed for. Recently upgraded pumps are capable of loading close to 1,000 gallons a minute to each diesel's belly tank, much faster than the 300-gallon-a-minute ability of yesterday's installation.

Save a bit here, save a bit there. Run faster trains!

Hardly has the last locomotive been replenished when a fourth train shows, bringing with it a rationale for those others marking time. Three big ones from Erie, their 12,000-hp purring in subdued tones, decelerate a maximum-sized stack train to a smartly executed halt. A train list depicts only 28 cars; each, however, is a well type equal to five ordinary car

No, this is not a service track set up in some yard but the mainline scene at Rawlins, Wyoming, as three westbounds occupy mainline tracks waiting to depart in serial fashion in UP's very typical fleeting practice on the main line.

length; or 140 at a more conventional measurement. West of North Platte, 28 is the limit, while to the east across the flatland of Nebraska, 35 such types are permitted to be coupled to locomotives. Considering that such trains routinely fly across the landscape at 70 mph, one can appreciate what UP is capable of.

Quickly, now—the anxiety quotient has been raised—a blue flag is raised to the lead unit's cab. Five minutes later a brief inspection has disclosed adequate fuel tank levels; the departing crew is aboard, the blue flag is down. Seconds tick off, then where two red orbs were stabbing the darkness there is one, the lower indication now displaying yellow. "Proceed on diverging route at prescribed speed through turnout."

Immediately, a locomotive bell sounds off as puffs of smoke lift from three exhaust stacks, a sign that inertia is already past tense.

No longer idle, traction motors soak up all the juice that GE's 16-cylinder design can muster. Gears revolve as they forcefully transmit energy to slowly accelerating wheelsets, six of them under each unit's frame. With 12,000 hp available, this race horse of a train won't lay back for long, though it is temporarily held in check by a 40-mph turnout. Long before midtrain, the red, yellow, green containers in vertical twos are bucking against that restriction, waiting only for that final straightening out as the last car slips through a switch. The leading unit is already close to 7,000 feet ahead on Laramie Subdivision iron, just waiting on the next throttle notch.

Ahead, green after green brightly reflects off 133-pound steel, seconded this summer night by miniaturized cab signals. Though momentarily redundant, they become a welcome companion when winter storms blanket western plains and mountains.

Relentlessly attacking space, the double stack is quickly miles ahead when the first of the three remaining movements receives its own emerald signal and rolls off toward the plateaus of western Wyoming. In succession the other two are sequenced into their schedules, probably as 50-mile-an-hour runs, given their makeup. They will stay in pursuit of each other till at least Green River, perhaps all the way to Salt Lake City.

Suddenly Rawlins is stilled. The sole voices are nearby street traffic and a pump transferring fuel from an oil refinery-sized storage tank owned by UP.

Not for long. Already other winking lights are wending their way across a console display, the one that's labeled Laramie Subdivision. They flash as they transmit this visual portrayal in miniature of three-dimensional railroading. Many trains haven't been to Rawlins yet, but they will be. Some are tomorrow's future, or the day after's, still waiting on a clearance to depart Stockton Yard, maybe rolling through the corn fields of rural Kansas or setting out from the great Northwest.

The way Union Pacific's map is laid out, most of them will show at Rawlins sometime, singly or in bunches.

Chief Organizer

Probably no major yard in the United States plays such a strategic role in systemwide train operations as UP's Bailey Yard in North Platte. Apart from a secondary route between Denver and Topeka, everything passing between UP's western domain and its eastern and southeastern districts must roll through North Platte.

More removed from metropolitan centers than most key facilities, it sprawls over 2,500 acres on the windswept prairie of western Nebraska. Two large hump yards, a mammoth diesel servicing and repair shop, plus general rolling stock maintenance combine to create the nation's largest single rail complex. Sixty, 70, even 80 trains rendezvous with North Platte every 24 hours—the ultimate concentration of train movements across the entire UP.

So extensive is this prairie facility that it has separate yardmasters for each direction, along with a general yardmaster. It is the place which takes butterflies (trains), turns them back into worms (cars) and then resurrects them into butterflies once again—on a grand scale. It is also UP's biggest remount station, where motive power changes on an assembly-line basis—say, 240–250 units a day.

The approach to either end of the yard features wide span signal bridges that display routing instructions for a half-dozen tracks. Often, while one or two trains are halted at either entrance waiting their turn to enter, a high-priority container train slips by on its way to the runthrough tracks that are themselves becoming busier with each passing year. Very few minutes pass without one of these priority movements hoving into view—in or outbound. They frequently come in bunches since this railroad likes to fleet its trains, especially the primary ones.

Wind has much to do with Bailey Yard's layout. Both automated classification yards, westward as well as eastward, have their retarders at the west end because of Nebaska's seasonal gusts, which flow from the west, and bowl tracks in both yards face east.

Not all trains can run through North Platte untouched, so computerized classification lists are already plugged into the system as a train arrives for working or rebuilding. The National Car System in St. Louis keeps tabs on each car as it moves across the entire UP–MoPac–MKT alliance, feeding instructions to yards throughout the West based upon reports it receives each time a train passes through a terminal, no matter how minor. Switch lists are well in hand long before a herder pulls the pin and the cars begin rolling through a series of grasping, clattering plates, setting the proper speed into each bowl track. The computer records how many cars are already in each track, calculating in its millisecond response how far each new entrant must roll to a coupling, addressing its momentum accordingly.

Parked on one of North Platte's two retarder yards, a two-unit set of SD40s is typical power assigned to hump yard service. This permanent assignment is indicated by the removal of the snowplow pilots.

Altogether there is a modest shortline railroad contained in Bailey Yard's seven-mile scene, 221 miles' worth. The westbound yard, opened for business in 1980, has 50 tracks in its bowl, while its opposite number is geared to a 64-track width. The latter is a bit more traditional in its spread as trains arrive to an eight-track receiving yard, go directly to the hump and, when categorized, are pulled out to a seven-track forwarding yard in the direction they will depart. Because the westward hump rolls cars to the east, its schematic is less standardized. The receiving yard lies south of the bowl; trains are pulled back west, humped east and then must be pulled east by a trim job—nomenclature for switch engines that clear the bowl—before being shoved back to a 10-track departure yard north of the bowl. Sounds a bit complex but the prairie winds are responsible.

Bailey's eastern perimeter houses a 13-track operation specializing in

With the arrival of GE's Dash-8 units en masse, the UP has taken on quite a different look from the days when the SD40s dominated. Here at the North Platte shop where running repairs are made, a couple of Dash-8s flank an earlier 3,000-hp GE unit.

the TOFC/COFC trade, with other runthrough tracks lying between the two humps as well as skirting around the north end.

Yet flexibility is a watchword, so that if any one section is full, arriving or departing runs will be assigned to any of the others. As a matter of fact, eastbound unit coal business has become so voluminous in recent times that its own specialized runthrough rails have proven inadequate, and many a unit coal move can be found changing power and crews in other Bailey yards. There is no clannishness here, just whatever it takes to run the terminal smoothly.

So extended and complex is this yard, there is a special overpass across the main line referred to as the "power lead." Exclusively for diesel locomotives, it allows them to cross from northside (westbound) tracks to the southside engine terminal without making time-consuming, intricate moves. A second lead crosses under the eastbound hump facility.

Given the volume of traffic passing through, one would expect a very large servicing/repair shop complex for locomotives. There are both, a large shop and plenty of servicing tracks for inspection and replenishment.

Eleven tracks lead through a cavernous building, normally crammed to its great folding doors with motive power in for repair. Usually a few dozen units are outside as well, waiting their turn unless they can be fixed without entering the shop itself. Sandwiched between the shop and the eastward bowl are another eight tracks of some length, routinely packed to the switch points with diesels just in off a train or listed for an outbound crew. A tall, towerlike structure houses a diesel service supervisor who monitors a daily average crowd of around 250 locomotives. They all re-

Opposite: Late on a summer's afternoon at North Platte, the lineup of outbound power stands ready for crews to arrive. The predominance of almost brand new power is obvious in the roof lines.

quire sand, fuel, lube oil along with a thorough inspection at the very least. For a sense of comparison, Hinkle, the northwest area's major terminal and the one closest to North Platte in importance, handles 2,300–2,400 total units in a month. North Platte does that in 10 days.

By the time you read this, North Platte dispatchers will be working out of Omaha, on one more set of panels in that extensive control center. During the summer of 1989 they were still housed at Bailey Yard, covering the great steel turnpike between Omaha and Cheyenne from five separate desks and two chief dispatchers. The newest of these stations displayed eight-year-old technology, the oldest, green metal panels and levers of 1950s' planning. No keyboard and cursor on these.

Those veteran dispatchers who had been around for years said they actually preferred the older machines with their throw levers for switches and signals. It was explained that under pressure you could actually work both hands at once, establishing routes by throwing manual controls in rapid-fire sequence, even simultaneous ones. Newer CTC panels of computer/keyboard technology had to be programmed sequentially, a minor idea to be sure, but illustrating the affinity one gains through long-term exposure to ideas. Traditions certainly die hard.

Now on most railroads, especially in single-track territory, such impressions might be labeled nitpicking. However, just looking over the shoulder of a DS working UP double-track or twin-track territory between Omaha and the West you can appreciate their needs. When a half-dozen trains of mixed importance begin to crowd in on a few milepost numbers you need all the dexterity allowable, even a two-handed router.

Another minor issue had to do with fleeting, a vital component of UP cross-country running advantage. A slight objection to computers was an inability to cancel a route within two control points of a train once that plan had been established, should slight alterations in performance subsequently occur. Once implemented the computer in North Platte had to run its course before a change could be punched in.

Page after page of eye-numbing statistics are really necessary to depict North Platte's place in Union Pacific's west. Some are fleetingly flashed in soft green style over the ever-present CRT screen, others in more durable paper and print. Regardless, they create an impression that Bailey Yard is like no other, on UP and probably anywhere else, certainly on western railroads.

Try symbol trains, for instance. Well over 200 are carded daily, from points west of North Platte to points east of North Platte, with a major fraction including "NP" at some point in their symbolism. In the road's present operating timetable, the shortest division is called the "North Platte," weighing in with a seemingly improbable 10 miles' worth of line, which is just about right for the center of attention. While it may be abbreviated in stature, Bailey Yard is wide in impact, the most important piece of UP's western architecture.

The Harriman line comes up near the original line over Sherman Hill at a place called Dale, where this trio of SD60s is seen under a late afternoon sky.

A Hill Called Sherman

Sherman Hill is an immense block of granite separating the plains of mid-America from Union Pacific's single-track empire. Its abrupt natural fence once generated one of the railroad's shorter crew districts, Cheyenne to Laramie. While helpers by the dozen plied the outbound tracks at Cheyene and drifted back downhill unburdened, the road freights they helped were typically slow, and many westbounds needed fresh crews at Laramie just a few dozen miles down the pike.

That was yesterday! In the early postwar period, UP reached a point where the number of train movements and contemporary construction techniques challenged the status quo in the form of a third track to be created along a new pathway. The original post-Civil War survey line had already been moved once, but this new line would lower the grade for westbounds, an important issue when proposed in the early 1950s.

Even the 4-8-8-4 class of *Big Boys* couldn't beat Sherman Hill with any kind of tonnage, generally requiring a 4-6-6-4 helper every time they blasted forth from the soot-stained yard at Cheyenne.

For all its reputation, Sherman Hill never was quite in the mold of Santa Fe's Raton or Southern Pacific's Tehachapi. At its worst, it offered a 1.55 percent maximum gradient along the eastern face from the summit at Sherman down into Cheyenne proper. Yet nowhere else on the westbound trek from Omaha to Ogden was more than an .82 percent gauntlet raised in a locomotive's face, and if these could be subjugated single-handedly, it seemed appropriate to downplay Sherman Hill to a similar standard. A parallel advantage lay in deleting helpers and their crews from the trainsheet.

This trio of mixed power, led by one of UP's "super engines," Dash-8 40C No. 9232, rolls down off Sherman Hill near Cheyenne, Wyoming.

Consequently, Sherman Hill was tackled and in a sense defeated before the diesel locomotive came along to dominate UP's main stem, for even as the new line came into being it was spoked-steel tires, not current driven wheels, that beat a steady tattoo along its 42½-mile length.

Realistically, complete dieselization was not far off. But when the new steel trail opened in 1953, steam engines peppered the Wyoming skyline in celebration—with soft coal from company-owned mines. Successive generations of internal combustion power would probably have done away with helpers, anyway, but UP has never been one to agonize over real needs, nor delay.

To keep the ruling grade within its target, construction forces hacked and filled their way across 42½ miles of new line, a length that although nine miles longer than the original, shaved time off the old westbound main. So the teeter-totter of a profile that exists between Laramie and Cheyenne became more symmetrical in terms of its impact upon train activities.

As a prototype of sorts, Sherman Hill is a different personality than others with which Union Pacific has daily contact. Windswept and barren for the most part, its natural bearing is not to be compared with Oregon's forested slopes or the tight defile of Feather River Canyon, where there is clearly but one line of advance to pursue. In natural contrast, Sherman Hill is quite open-minded, modestly bald in look, and although steep in the crossed hairs of a surveyor's transit, capable of alternative approaches as the 1950s' line addition aptly demonstrated.

Running south of the pre-1950s double track, the Sherman Hill Relocation, as it came to be known, is a predominantly westbound alley, while the original line serves eastbound traffic and/or light van/stack trains on occasion.

Like the rest of this railroad and especially over its mid-America trunk, there are spasms of activity mixed in with interludes of relative silence. While it would be nice if action were more evenly spaced across a clock face, no major railroad can function that way in modern times. When your major competition is burning rubber out of Chicago or Oakland in early evening, how long before sand must flow between steel on steel?

If this is happening in all principal cities just about the same time, then deal with it, or learn to spell MEDIOCRITY, not RAILROADING.

Sherman Hill is not such an expression, nor is anywhere west of Omaha. Yesteryear's fanciful vision is not 1990s' reality.

A mild scent of grease, a few twinges of infrared radiation represent 28 five-car cuts of colorful stacked containers in what are fast becoming ubiquitous well cars in for a crew's quick change at Cheyenne's brownstone depot. Odds are pretty fair that an eastbound of lesser status will be held outside of town, or perhaps even another westbound will be kept in check on an adjacent track while three GE titans head for Sherman Hill with their 12,000-hp under charter.

From ground level, those red, orange and green-hued metal storage boxes stretch to infinity. Yet, well before the blunt reflection of a final portable bin has passed, motive power has slipped past a pair of crossovers to the south line heading straight for Speer, where a connection with Denver is fashioned. Then begins a looping, meandering course across fills as high as 157 feet, cuts that exceed 100 feet from top to a 40-foot-wide floor.

The pace drops off quickly and sounds of struggle replace those of customary breakneck speed, which have been the stack train's lot across so many subdivisions till now. Not to worry, though, for Omaha's computer has been in touch, settling upon those burly Dash-8s to get the job done. And the "Bunker" is always there to monitor progress.

Other than its approach at either extreme, the South Line is rarely in sight of the original main line, blocked off by several miles of intervening hilltop. And while the stack train chips away consistently at altitude, eastbounds are easing over the old crest at Sherman and drifting through a controlled descent toward Cheyenne and the comparatively easy running that lies across a now horizontal skyline.

There are plenty of light trains on the parade ground, too. Piggybackers, perhaps, kept lean by design, and if the South Line is bunched these can easily take the original route on their way west, or eastbounds can be shunted around each other. Given the territory, today's creation of Sherman Hill is about as state-of-the-art as can be conceived.

As for tomorrow . . . well, that is a different story.

Slightly west of Dale on the old line, a meeting of track diagrams takes place, and for approximately three mileposts everything that crosses between Laramie and Cheyenne is in consort. Then at Hermosa, tracks separate again with westbounds taking a southerly single track, as eastbounds stick to the north as they come through Laramie to tackle the hill.

Climbing up the western face of Sherman Hill in summer's clear weather, a general freight is pulled by the now older power on a UP roster. Were it a piggybacker or stack train, more up-to-date diesel models would be on the point.

Interestingly enough, just outside Laramie one can often glimpse two or three trains at a time on both old and new paths. Slipping downgrade, a westbound is rolling toward town while up on the grassy slopes yellow diesels in both directions ply their heavy-duty trade. Such opportunities are definitely slim on the other side except close in to Cheyenne where everything rolls under a Burlington Northern line as it comes overhead on a steel bridge.

Sherman Hill's space is busier than anywhere else; in fact, it is the only link in the entire east-west chain that every diesel, every freight car must roll through. And while not much traffic does it, a few trains can avoid Cheyenne by way of Denver. No such option attends Sherman Hill anywhere to the west; its hectic train sheet approximates just about any subdivision on that thousand miles' worth of double track. Somehow, though, like all mountain subs, the Wyoming upthrust looks busier than either flank, primarily because its gradient slows the tempo to a walk for some, a gait for others.

While high-class candidates for speed have little trouble in topping Sherman Hill with their light charges, heftier trains—call 'em drags if you will—can be seen struggling toward Dale or Sherman at a snail's pace.

Coupled to enough motive power on the point to get the job done, these latter aren't in any pressure cooker; they'll get across in due time. Mastering the .82 percent here means that they will do it everywhere else as well. Slipping out of Nebraska, through Cheyenne and over Sherman delivers Union Pacific into territory very much on the up-and-down concept that has sustained the railroad in the six-axled category of prime movers.

It is not as if one subdivision follows another in seamless fashion, for each has a distinctive trademark, in both name and topography. Union Pacific is sculpted into discernible zones, east of North Platte, the single-track dominion, the Northwest, and so forth. This adds to one widespread system where each part displays its own dynamic.

That huge hunk of granite overlooking the great plains? There is only one Sherman Hill, no matter how many ways you carve it!

A great cloud of diesel smoke surrounds a train on Sherman Hill as it pops from a tunnel near Hermosa.

Engine servicing facilities at Council Bluffs, Iowa.

One Section's Profile

Council Bluffs, Iowa, just across the Missouri River from Omaha, is UP's sally port to the West, but not its busiest terminal. That status is reserved for North Platte, a couple of hundred miles inside the system.

Much of today's traffic is high-wheeling, especially the intermodal clones. They roll through terminals and cross subdivisions almost as fast, if not quicker, than the passenger runs of yesteryear. There are no people to hustle aboard, no conductors fidgeting at some last-second delay, just a crew who rides a locomotive. So when a train pulls out, it accelerates to its utmost; by the time mid-train is passing an observer it is already going 30–35 mph. No slowing for a caboose here. If there are a dozen terminals on a transcontinental trip, this means a savings of 4–5 minutes each, perhaps an overall hour between Chicago, Los Angeles, Portland, or Seattle.

Just *get on and go* is the watchword of the fast ones!

Unlike the stack trains, which connect with the C&NW here in Fremont, Nebraska, this eastbound train is staying on UP rails as it heads for Council Bluffs.

In dispatching lingo, the twin-track span between Council Bluffs–North Platte is "fast track"; in engineers' parlance it is all *Run 8* territory. Once westbounds top a hill through Omaha's suburbs, they're out of the starting gate. Slender steel bands of steel gapped to a four-foot, 8½-inch width are flatter here than out beyond the Rockies, and this is where UP can make time. Here is Rule 251 territory, the equivalent of run until overtaken, so if nothing gets in your way—it won't for Z trains—the green blocks appear in never-ending sequence.

This segment of the turnpike is characterized by generally flat, tangent gaps tied together with subtle, gently curving arcs. While roadbed is already climbing toward the Continental Divide, it is so trifling per mile as to not register on multiple lashups of energetic diesels.

Perhaps a third of what moves through North Platte will circulate by way of Council Bluffs; another third owes its existence from the C&NW link at Fremont, while the balance is by way of Kansas City ties. So as you go west the number of train movements builds, and builds.

Fremont is 40 miles into the Council Bluffs Subdivision, the latter a 282-mile part of the great east-west main. The town lies about an overnight run away from the great Chicago rail center, so westbound hotshots tend to crowd the rails in early-morning clusters while the eastbound parade comes along later in the day, due into the Windy City early on the following A.M. Given today's time-sensitive, demanding traffic, which is typically dependent upon big-city pairings, the fast train's routine rarely varies by more than a few moments from one day to the next.

Little doubt is left about the two roads' cooperative effort out of Fremont, as a new yard office sports the flags of both roads as well as a stone billboard with their logos. On the road a very commonplace sight is a C&NW GP50 leading a stack or trailer train. Some North Western units come with cab signals allowing them to work the point on UP trains, one of the few instances where other than armour yellow is out front. C&NW also features automatic train stop on its own territory, something UP doesn't have but is considering for future installation.

So it is that with quick grace a westbound pig train clatters across the connecting steel bands at Fremont and onto UP iron. C&NW is no longer calling the shots; Union Pacific is now in command.

Irregular splashes of lightning illuminate peripheral cloud decks in a post-midnight setting as the initial cab signal indications cast a dim glow across an engineer's control stand, confirming what the wayside lights are saying.

"Green board," the hogger calls out to no one in particular, though a silhouetted figure peering out the opposite cab window nods in expectant concurrence. What else comes with a call to ride a Canal Street–North Platte Z train?

Air . . . 90 pounds and holding steady.

Throttle . . . Run 6 on its way to Run 8. There is running room now,

DAVID HARUM
KENT
UNION PACIFIC
3409

just about 250 miles before North Platte's chattering three-ring circus takes over as dawn spreads across the prairie.

The timetable says that 70 mph is an appropriate pace; only here or there is a lesser number desirable, through a town perhaps, at a grade crossing (with the BN in three instances). Otherwise, sustained speed, the flavor of modern railroading, is captured in unending fashion. Two 4,000-hp titans, locked in elephant-like embrace, master the darkened plains of Nebraska, climbing just a bit toward a western crest still far off.

With commonplace occurrence, firefly-sized lights appear at a distant front, grow to headlight-sized orbs, and in the briefest of moments flash by toward places that now lie behind. Long cuts of spindly 89-foot steel flats, perhaps heavily loaded coal cars, trail diesel exhaust, laid perpendicular at the moment of exit by rushing wind.

On occasion a slower train has taken one of those center-style sidings; in other instances, one might be off to the side possibly switching an industry or perhaps picking up a half-dozen loaded hog cars for the West Coast. It is a bit startling to hear a dispatcher come over the radio, instructing a crew to stop for "hog cars." Shades of yesterday and a different West. Union Pacific says it makes money, so why not?

Routinely, UP expects and demands it that way. Trains sprint past planted fields, through darkened towns and toward the next crew-change stop, then the one beyond that and on to a series of etceteras. The symbols to which they respond, CSSEZ (Canal Street–Seattle) or OANP (Oakland–North Platte) explain their missions.

Just at dawn, as the first sun rays creep over a horizon, our westbound van train is threading the receiving yard at North Platte, just another of the 70–80 through movements that cruise through here daily.

Further on, while mileposts unfold in three-digit sequence, scenery fetches a different look around those twin trails of steel. Corn fields give way to grasslands; eventually a great granite block called Sherman Hill stands tall, and beyond that, visions of a pioneering West, created in terms of plateau and mesa topped off with vast cloud-bedecked skies. Only tiny steam locomotives and gun-belted cowboys are missing.

Each part of the package that is Union Pacific is contoured distinctively, uniquely in its own image. Yet from an operating standpoint all should prove uniform, as from a copy machine. The same locomotives, the same rolling stock, the same rules of the game, prevail between whatever destinations are spit out.

That the pace of action varies from one subdivision to another is geographical in scope, expectations notwithstanding. To create the best performance with the tools at hand is what each era's railroading is all about. And if you can build a better implement than your competitor, that helps too.

As for Union Pacific, that tool just happens to be the great steel turnpike. It is well employed without exception.

Opposite: Racing through Lexington, Nebraska, a hotshot heads east, probably for a C&NW connection at Fremont, Nebraska. Its consist stamps it as a "Z" type train.

6018
6018
UNION PACIFIC

THE COAL TRADE

IN THE MID-1970s, today's North Platte Subdivision was a shrinking branch with a grand total of two to three casual trains a week. An outbound crew to the end of that gradually rusting line often waited two days for a return call. Union Pacific was considering abandonment.

A turnaround came from the oil crisis, which boosted demand for western coal dramatically. UP found it was in a strategic position to cash in on the coal trade. In 1982–83 it forged a joint effort, primarily with Chicago and North Western, to move diggings in the Powder River Basin, Wyoming's most abundant coal source. Today, this source, plus others in southern Wyoming, southern Illinois and Utah's Carbon County provide UP with almost 35 percent of its annual gross-ton miles.

The revived North Platte line is now reaching maximum capacity; it caters to 30 to 35 trains every 24-hour period in a cooperative effort with the Burlington Northern and the Chicago and North Western. Where once a train crew felt lucky to achieve a two-day turnaround, today's seniority roster lists 40 pool crews, many of whom rarely wait long for a trip following their mandatory rest. In fact, although this coal run is only about 168 miles long, it is routinely tied up short on the hours-of-service law, so dense are train movements. Nor is it unusual to hit every siding along the way for at least one or more opposing trains.

Coal haulage is a balanced activity. As a dispatcher comments, "For every empty train that heads into the sub an equal-sized one comes out." Sort of UP's law of physics: for every action there is an equal and opposite reaction.

A major proportion of coal tonnage moves in solid consists, often unit trains, although in UP nomenclature the distinction of "unit" is reserved for dedicated sets of rolling stock. A hundred cars of a total coal train made up from pool equipment must stay in that business without being broken up at the end of its run to meet the criteria.

A single unit-train schedule may involve several sets of rolling stock. Many trains, especially those on the North Platte Sub, are privately owned

Opposite: Typical of UP's modern-day coal business is this IPPX train rolling through Rio Grande territory and onto UP rail at Provo, Utah, for final delivery.

by the utility companies they serve. If you assume a five- to six-day turnaround on some round trips, or if the train involved is a daily one, then you need that many individual sets of cars. Of course, not all such movements pass through the mines daily, but you can visualize the multiple groups of huge, coal-filled hoppers running under a single private label, a solo roll call.

Rolling stock is not the only consideration affecting the coal trade. Because there can be two or three mines supplying coal to a single unit train, the loading site on each trip may be a different one. The ultimate user, typically with Wyoming coal, is probably a power plant with varying stockpile requirements in the Midwest or Southwest. Often a train is parked for a time to adjust to those needs.

For the railroad, full equipment utilization can be a continuing variable. Consider Mopac's stable planning process in southern Illinois.

Several unit trains circulate among five principal mines in the region. What a mine loads, and when, is determined by the size and quality of the utility's present stockpile. Black diamonds vary considerably in moisture, sulfur and energy content, all factors that buyers must consider and pass onto the railroads as they evaluate their transportation requirements.

Holidays may affect other parts of the Union Pacific but not the North Platte line. In fact, sometimes a dispatcher notes more action on those days than on a regular workday. Another unique feature is the egalitarianism of the route. Here all trains are created equal, and empties have as much right as loads. Also well practiced is the "fleeting" concept, with three or four movements running close behind one another in a single pack. There is nothing unusual about a brimful train holing up for empties if it's the best decision. Back at the Harriman Dispatching Center a trio of colored arrows may be crowding one another across a flat glass screen in a tight formation not routinely practiced elsewhere on Union Pacific as coal trains pack the line.

That background explained, let's take a look at some of the hottest single-track dramatics anywhere. It certainly adds up the heaviest, as well.

It is precisely 1533 hours on a late September day in 1989 as a teleprinter in the yard office at South Morrill, Nebraska, begins to click out the next 24-hour train sheet for this coal-based yard. Blocked into eastbound and westbound sections, the coming events reflect normalcy, at least momentarily.

The intrigue begins with the 4 P.M. arrival of westbound C&NW units powering an empty. The two roads pool a fair amount of locomotives in this area, and No. 5013, a C&NW SD50, is holding down the lead in a two-unit lashup. Ten minutes later a second train is supposed to be approaching the yard limit sign in South Morrill. Six more empty trains should be there at 10 P.M., followed by a four-hour lull. Then the westbound parade resumes between 2:30 A.M. and 1:30 P.M. with another 10 movements.

Two early series SD50s are back on Union Pacific track as they roll west through downtown Omaha with a unit coal train. Remnants of the old passenger station that served Burlington and Rock Island passenger trains in years past is seen to the right.

Curiously enough, while the lineups themselves are spit forth on the traditional 12-hour clock, the schedules accompanying each set of train orders use a 2400 standard, the familiar "Zulu Time" of military operations.

These days, every train on Union Pacific is "scheduled," that is, a complete printout from origin to final destination is issued with train orders at every terminal. True, the slower ones often slip a bit, but it has become an article of faith that nothing penetrates mainline iron without a statement of its proposed performance.

The westbound lineup also alludes to five potential departures from North Platte's ever busy terminal. One is holding, one is stored and three are building, according to the printout. The so-called "building" moves are probably being fashioned from UP pool equipment in response to a particular need, while the holding train just hasn't been scheduled yet. "Stores, NOP" is probably a private label waiting for access to a mine where it can be filled, perhaps in a day or so. Right now the mine is not quite ready for its vacant hoppers.

Of 18 westbounds listed, four will have C&NW power leading. The balance will come along behind armour-yellow units, and one-third of them will be handled by a single SD60—traditional cab, or wide-nosed variant. Empties typically weigh in at 3,000–3,500 tons; a more notable circumstance is an eastbound assignment where one prime mover may trudge along with 14,000 tons as a normal allotment.

One might think that 10,000 tons of trainline would prove to be more than ample for even two units, but UP has found its SD60s to be tough engines. In fact, no trainman can remember handling a light train like that in the past five years. The typical eastbound move is 14,000–15,000 tons spread over 6,100 feet. Timewise, the average eastbound trip would be about eight hours, and the average westbound about 10 to 12 hours. And despite computers and CTC, some dispatchers are said to unconsciously favor empties over loads, and vice versa. (Though hard to believe, some trainmen who work a particular section of railroad claim they can tell who's pushing the buttons by their train's behavior.)

Returning to South Morrill's midafternoon lineup, the eastbound section begins with a scheduled departure at 12:45 P.M. of the CNANW symbol, a typical coal train with 112 cars carrying 14,560 tons. On the point is No. 6163, one of EMD's unparalleled weightlifters. While other engines may appear in cameo, it is the 3,800-hp boys who will be hauling the bulk of coal on Union Pacific for years to come.

After the CNANW symbol, nine more heavy haulers will be sent on their way toward North Platte, the last one rolling out at 10 P.M. Momentarily, this eastbound scheme doesn't stretch beyond the late evening, but don't believe there's nothing on the horizon. It is just that UP has a better handle on its empty movements since they're all on the system, while the C&NW dispatcher may not have updated its partner yet on the inbounds. Later on, say around 2100 hours, the list will be crowded with more outbounds.

So if we take just the day's segment between the 12:40 P.M. departure of an eastbound hauler and the last inbound empty at 10:30 P.M.—ignoring those moves listed past midnight—we are looking at 18 full-fledged trains. Nor does this take into account the link with Burlington Northern connections at Northport, 113 miles west of O'Fallons where this subdivision joins the main line. Many of the BN units on North Platte's servicing tracks are coal-train workers paired with armour-yellow ones in a pool. Generally speaking, three units arrive in Northport from BN's west, and perhaps a single UP unit will be assigned east of there. Quite a contrast when a solo SD60M takes over from a trio of mixed GEs/EMDs off the Powder River line of BN. Adding to the heavy volume of coal, the BN–UP dialogue may produce another 10 or so daily trains, split as always 50-50 in appearance.

While CTC controls the roadbed to Northport, the additional 47 miles west to South Morrill are equipped with automatic block signals and track warrant control. Even though UP's standard 133-pound rail is used, train speeds on the North Platte Subdivision have until just recently been restricted to a 40-mph maximum. Now, however, coal trains are allowed

The partnership between UP and C&NW in the coal trade is best illustrated by this service track scene at South Morrill, Nebraska, where the lines interchange up to 30 trains a day, split quite naturally 50-50 between loaded and empty runs.

to run at 50 mph. The pacing item for coal tonnage is arrival when expected; speed and a fast turnaround are not crucial.

For instance, we find that a coal train symbolized as CNWNA leaves Independence, Arkansas, at 1600 hours on Day 1, taking with it a host of empties back to Wyoming for a reload. With scheduled layovers at intermittent points, it will be rolling through the suburbs of Kansas City around midnight on Day 2. North Platte's terminal is a suppertime call on Day 3 and at 0230 hours on Day 4 UP will be calling upon C&NW to take over the baton at South Morrill. By contrast, the total elapsed time is roughly equal to that permitted for the Los Angeles–Canal Street Z to go between Los Angeles and Chicago.

Each train has its place on the railroad. Each will be expected to perform accordingly.

As it passes through North Platte, a coal train will receive its basic diagnostic checkup, the thousand-mile inspection. Perhaps not all but certainly the bulk of such schedules require examination. While North Platte has several runthrough tracks set aside exclusively for coal business, other general yard tracks are also used. A fuel rack attached to the runthrough rails allows engines to be replenished while trains are being inspected.

In terms of physical characteristics, the North Platte Sub is level Nebraska farmland or cattle-grazing country. Not that UP minds, for this allows a single SD60 to handle those 14,000-ton trains into North Platte with relative ease, if not speed. There is a slight downgrade toward O'Fallons, with its direction favoring loads.

Of more significance than gradient is the wind, particularly each spring. The dust-strewn, wind-blown prairie is a real-life situation well known to UP. As seasonal breezes escalate, trains slow accordingly, mainly the empties. The critical figure is in the vicinity of 30 mph; anything there or above calls for two units instead of one on light trains, while loaded ones barely notice what is happening. Buffeted and rocked by grassland winds, westbounds are often slowed to a flatout pace of 20 mph as they creep toward South Morrill.

Beyond Northport, to the other side of South Morrill, both Burlington Northern and Chicago and North Western are not so fortunate in their track profiles as UP. The landscape gradually changes to low-lying hills, requiring an attachment of more power. The BN here has its standard mixes of both GE and EMD six-axled models, while C&NW holds forth with SD50s and 60s, along with a recently delivered class of GE Dash 8-40Cs.

In spite of the weather, coal haulage proceeds at a steady, constant pace. Even severe-winter weather has little effect, at least not on tonnage. Where mainline trains on the steel turnpike might be reduced during very low temperatures, coal moves along unaffected. Years ago when friction bearings were the rule on rolling stock, extremely low thermometer readings led to shortened trains, essentially because of greater resistance at the axle. Today, cold weather primarily causes sluggish train lines, but that has little impact on coal trains whose uniform equipment is not from different sources with varying maintenance and age. Brake systems are operated at 90 pounds between North Platte and South Morrill; 80 pounds east of UP's huge terminal.

Matching a set of train orders on a hotshot with that of a coal train yields an interesting comparison in optimum horsepower. In territory west of North Platte "Z"-designated runs typically will demand four hp for every ton they carry, reduced to a three-to-one ratio east across the flatlands of Nebraska. Coal trains by contrast carry no such figures. If they did, it would be how many tons per horsepower. Even with a set of three SD60s hauling mainline-originated trains out of Hanna in southern Wyoming, a 14,000-ton train would exceed 3,800 hp times three in anyone's math!

One development currently under consideration in the coal trade is the utilization of aluminum hoppers. The railroad presently owns about 550 of these lightweights. Each of these cars comes across at approximately half the weight of an all-steel example, though it must have a traditional steel frame for the heavy pounding that it incurs. Because they project lower maintenance costs and can tote a heavier revenue load as a complete train, these cars may become tomorrow's standard. A locomotive that can muscle 110 steel cars can take on 120 aluminum ones, improving its hauling ability from 11,000 to 12,000 tons. Over a long period of years that can prove to be important.

Handling coal is more complex than imagined. For instance, some aluminum cars assigned to service out of Powder River Basin are unpainted; those on the Wasatch Mountain slopes in Utah are black. This difference has to do with the higher moisture content in the far western coal, which can freeze in a few hours, while loads moving off the North Platte Sub can go for days without that happening. Just a bit of paint can make a difference in heat absorption. Frozen loads have to be lanced with stem probes or pass through a car shaker, shortening a car's lifespan if done too often.

Coal off the North Platte Sub principally moves east through the Omaha–Council Bluffs area or down through Marysville, Kansas, then on to Kansas City to MoPac, or other links. Mostly, the mines in this area feed utilities in Kansas, Arkansas, and Texas. A bit of trainmen's nomenclature refers to them as "Jukes," an acronym derived from an early unit train which ran under the banner, JEFFERSON UTILITY, KANSAS EAST.

UP's on-line coal is mostly clustered in western Wyoming, particularly around Hanna. Here, a trio of mines, Rosebed Coal Sales and Medicine Bow Mine of the surface variety and Cyprus Shoshone Coal Corporation of underground status, work from a plateau overlooking UP's main line.

Empties and loads meet in the coal yard at North Platte, on the tracks specifically set aside for that business. In the background, a slow freight identified by older power on the point sets out for the West.

Working through the streets of San Pedro, California, in 1988, a unit coal train out of Utah heads for shipside. Looming in the background is one of the U.S. Navy's *Aegis* class cruisers in drydock at the Todd Shipyard.

The Ramsey Spur, a five-mile connecting track, lifts upward from the fast-running main stem to tap this coal field. Mindful of Sherman Hill's barrier near Cheyenne and the undulating mixture of mesa and plateau in the opposite direction, no single unit, not even an SD60, can work this assignment alone, so a typical coal run will find three units of new heavy-duty power attached to its couplers.

Another source of coal is Wyoming's Kemmerer Branch, a step off the turnpike toward the northwest. Often there's a set of power idling at Kemmerer, waiting to go down a nearby 10-mile stub to trade empties for a string of loaded hoppers. (An additional heavy traffic item from this location is molten sulfur, evidenced by a large number of tank cars labeled for that product.)

Just about the time UP began funneling coal trains into its system from Northport, then South Morrill, the West Coast export market started to bloom. Coal for export, principally through the port of San Pedro in Southern California, generally originates from on-line mines in western Wyoming or via the Rio Grande/Utah Railway interchange at Provo, Utah.

You can always tell when a coal ship is in San Pedro because the number of solid hopper loans/empties moving across the Utah and California Divisions reaches a frenzied peak, dominating the types of trains seen over several days.

Amid the piers and massive architecture of L.A.'s modern port complex, dust-bound conveyors and clanking machinery quickly reduce full-

Climbing out from Cima Hill in 1988, the LACSZ passes by a waiting coal train to the left while to the right another freight heading in the same direction—toward Las Vegas—will soon be passed.

sized trains to empty shells, setting the stage for a return journey back to the mines or into pool service.

Such is the coal trade, action and reaction.

Mixed in with general traffic elsewhere, coal trains are not as dominant a force as on the North Platte Subdivision. Still, they are plentiful and their expansion continues as a welcome addition to business. It seems that hardly a month goes by without the railroad contracting to move more hoppers on a steady, programmed basis.

Although Union Pacific may not have the reputation as a coal hauler in the same sense as a Burlington Northern or a CSX, that may change.

On any day UP will be calling crews to duty for roughly 30–35 unit trains of its own permanent origins, not counting interchange. The bulk will be coal and grain, while many others with a facade of gons or hoppers will be just another train. The mere assemblage of a hundred hoppers in a onetime movement, say to shipside in Southern California, will not qualify.

In many instances a unit train is composed of customer-owned rolling stock, primarily in coal haulage, while railroad-owned cars are mostly used in the grain trade.

While generally not applicable to coal, the concept of "unit" in grain means anything more than 20-car cuts, meaning that four or five of them in dedicated service could add to a solid movement.

Fourteen thousand covered hoppers, primarily Union Pacific but including some private brand markings, are assigned to the grain pool. Other cars are drawn into this group as needed, moving out when their job is done. Unlike the coal business, which tends to be more consistent, grain often alternates between a surplus of rolling stock to a shortage in a few weeks. There is also a varying U.S. agricultural outlook from year to year.

The majority of grain is intended for export, zeroing in mostly on northwest ports for transshipment to massive oceangoing vessels. At Coloma, a small port up the Columbia River from Portland, facilities exist that can empty a 100-car grain train in three hours. Some 70 percent of all grain moves in less than 20-car lots, collated into 100-car dimensions for handling.

Forty-eight hours' pre-notification is a compulsory demand at present, even for *ad hoc* grain trains. Power must be lined up, customer needs catalogued and a schedule determined. Very little runs across Union Pacific these days without some kind of agenda punched into electronic circuitry. Revealed on the bunker wall at Omaha, the master's voice is depicted in train symbols and lights that link control point to control point in parade fashion across thousands of miniature miles.

Wide-cab SD60M No. 6149 leads a trio of older SD40s on an empty coal train bound for reloading in the Hanna and Medicine Bow area. Green River, Wyoming, 1989.

Laramie, Wyoming, and Sherman Hill lie ahead of this unit coal train out of Hanna so a triple lashup of big SD60Ms is called for.

Coal trains require a five-day prior scheduling window, a comfortable lead time that is not difficult to arrange in their case.

Shippers, particularly in the grain business where they tend to be smaller, habitually overbook equipment to ensure its availability. Naturally, the railroad tries to discourage this practice so tariffs or penalties are adjusted to balance these requirements.

Soda ash, coiled-steel rolls and iron ore represent other unit-train identities. In one of the longest such runs, coiled-steel billets in low-sided gondolas circulate cross-country between a mill in Pennsylvania and Pittsburg, California. Here a finishing plant is dependent on the railroad for timely delivery of its raw material. It must not be disappointed.

The area around Green River, Wyoming, goes by the label, SODA ASH PATCH, known for the mineral it produces by the trainload. Several well-known chemical companies mine local deposits. Typically, a pair of solid soda ash trains leave Green River's mesa-shadowed yard for North Platte on a daily basis, while a similar train departs every other day for West Coast destinations.

A recent list indicated an eastbound soda ash symbol with 173 loads, five empties. Total tonnage, 21,611!

A load/load concept is generated by certain iron ore movements, bringing a smile to those who count revenue. Eastbound coal is hauled to Chicago, while a return trip handles iron ore pellets to the Columbia

Geneva steel mill outside Provo, Utah. Naturally such traffic is variable, but perhaps 15 trains operate a month, picking up their ore from the Mesabi Range in upper Minnesota. Another 12 trains per month may flow out of an ore source near Cedar City in southern Utah to the same locale near Provo.

In summary, the unit coal train is bursting seams on UP's North Platte Subdivision in western Nebraska. Such business elsewhere would definitely be welcome news.

Not far east of North Platte a unit coal train with aluminum-sided cars heads down the great steel turnpike with Kansas City and a Southwest power plant in mind.

Union Pacific's western coal field producers are found in concert with Rio Grande and Utah Railway interchange at Provo, Utah. Labor Day, 1989, finds new power from UP and used power from Utah Railway rubbing noses in Provo.

Locked in partnership, UP and BN units leave the twin-tracked main west of North Platte to begin their run down the North Platte Subdivision and a refill at Powder River Basin mines.

Railroad Yard
421A
6061
6061

ALONG THE SOUTHERN EDGE

TWO MAJOR DEVELOPMENTS have contributed to a very important role for the North Platte–Kansas City line. One is the development of coal out of Powder River Basin mines; the second is acquisition of the Missouri Pacific. Both have generated a current-day performance equal to that of any other single-track section on Union Pacific.

Throughout its far-flung western empire, Union Pacific serves one truly great railroad terminal area, Kansas City. While the railroad has created grand yards like North Platte and Hinkle, those are outposts of a sort, key to home road needs but unaligned with nearby yards of other railroads. Although the West Coast cities generate interchange activity, none of it occurs on a scale associated with a clustering of other carriers. And though some independent names have disappeared through consolidation or merger, Kansas City is the one place in UP's west where full trainloads are routinely exchanged between participants. Second only to Chicago as a national rail crossroads, it is surrounded by a great agricultural belt of high plains which generate thousands of annual trains. In terms of connections to just about everywhere east or west, it is the rail equivalent of a full freeway cloverleaf.

Prior to acquiring MoPac, the UP was centered upon the Kansas City, Kansas side but now is all over town, including what was once M-K-T's yard tracks.

With 60 miles of terminal complexity under its belt, UP's Kansas City Division is a jigsaw puzzle of roadbed. Everybody's power is seen in everyone else's yard limits, what with great volumes of interchange and the now commonplace schedules of runthroughs. Two or three years ago you might have seen a lot of foreign road power on UP, but with its recent massive purchase of new power little gets past North Platte except C&NW units.

To a person unfamiliar with its intricacies, a terminal area will seem an unfathomable maze of switches, connecting junctions and signals, with a hundred different routing possibilities. The twin Kansas Cities are no exception. Presumably by sitting down at a table with maps and devoting

Opposite: Kansas City, like Chicago, has a giant complex of yard tracks to conquer. On the Kansas side of this two-state railroad sprawl, a UP coal train works its way west toward Marysville and, eventually, North Platte.

careful attention to their legends the maze would prove of reasonable ownership, while long-standing experience in towers and engine cabs makes it work. All sorts of trains scurry from one yard to another, while obvious trunkline movements sort their way through a puzzling layout. Interchange runs are omnipresent with air horns braying their impatient demands upon some nearby tower in an unending chorus.

With UP, MoPac and now M-K-T working as one, a home road advantage through this terminal has been born. Santa Fe has long benefited from it, shortening terminal delay so long associated with a hand off between separate lines. Now UP's hands extend to both sides of this far-flung terminal.

Armstrong Yard on the Kansas side of this vast complex has long been UP's final destination. From here the long trains set out for North Platte or along the southern line into eastern Colorado and Denver. Now Armstrong and West Yard, a modest-sized facility farther out on the edge of town, have been joined to Neff Yard, MoPac's principal area terminal. Where once armour yellow meant connections only west of Kansas City, it now radiates to all parts of the compass except northeast. As a consequence, the flow of trains has increased markedly between the previously independent systems, most visually in coal-train traffic with the blunt-nosed SD60s running well east into former MOP territory. As of now, the Dash-8s are kept west of Omaha while all the SD40s from both roads have been combined in one giant numbering series. The ex-MP units are usually discernible because many won't exhibit dynamic brake pods, something UP would never do without.

While movements into and beyond Neff Yard can be parceled out across five separate subdivisions, on the west there is only one, the Marysville Sub, the longtime UP portal into Kansas. In terms of density it rivals any other heavy-duty single-track section on the entire railroad. Always important as a traffic source, its significance has reached new heights with Wyoming coal, and it's the logical link through Kansas City, improved with the fusing of MoPac's southwest system. Much of today's coal is headed into that region to fuel power plants.

The Marysville Sub is a long one, close to 300 miles in span, linking Kansas City with Gibbon Junction where the twin-track trunk across Nebraska is encountered. Roughly 30 of the 70 or so trains that run east of North Platte's Bailey Yard will polish the switch points at CP175, the entrance to Marysville Sub at Gibbon Junction.

Rule 251 dominates the initial 45 miles of twin tracks beyond Kansas City's West Yard. Sprawling suburbs are quickly left behind, revealing everyone's vision of Kansas: farms, farms and more farms. Grain silos point their cylindrical shapes skyward, singly and in long clusters. Tank cars cluster around bulk unloading facilities, which are legion, while feed stores and tractor dealerships back up to the tracks in many small towns. Although unit-coal runs and high-profile container types have little truck

At Kansas City's terminal area, an empty coal train rolls toward Kansas Division territory.

with such pedestrian scenes, many solid grain trains heading for Pacific or Gulf Coast ports take their first step locally.

To a racing train, urgently connecting the big cities and important harbors of America, these unpretentious communities are mere signposts, an endless clutter of crossing signals bringing home a train's own roar, suddenly apparent, ricocheting off a few blocks of packed buildings before open countryside is regained. That small dot of light ahead quickly turns into an opposing movement closing at equal velocity, 140 mph combined when both trains are striding along at the 70-mph standard so widely achieved on this railroad.

Scattered among fellow roster members along the way are some in red and grey bearing numbers not usually found cabside on those of yellow dress, for Southern Pacific now speeds across Kansas and into its own yard, Armourdale, in the Kansas City labyrinth. Having acquired Rock Island's onetime Golden State Route beyond Tucumcari, the Espee now utilizes trackage rights from Topeka on into Kansas City, packing more movement in the lower end of Marysville Sub.

As a means of gathering matters under control, the final 10 miles of twin track through Topeka's forest of grain elevators revert to CTC, since a solo set of ribbons dominates the next 200 miles. Topeka is a stereotype of Kansas: the huge grain elevators, hundreds of covered hoppers scattered in a half-dozen nearby yards and ongoing local action involving small diesels. Hardly ever is there a silent railroad moment, for somewhere in town, either on UP or the other major tenant, Santa Fe, something is working. A switcher is shuttling cars beneath the shadows of a grain silo while nearby the bang-bang of a local making up shakes dust and sends pigeons flying. Quietly slipping by on more important tasks, the big city types with their unit-coal train look or solid trailer flats rather ignore this provincial enterprise, as theirs is a higher calling. And if they should meet out there in a world of mainline labors there is little doubt as to who will step aside.

A metal sign and controlled switch indicate West Menoken, where the easily dispatched set of twin tracks west of Kansas City narrow to one. The rural, cross-farm trek of the Marysville Sub has begun.

Sidings average about eight miles apart hereabouts, not including a 10-mile section of double track to either side of Marysville, the midpoint where crews trade off. Because of heavy traffic, sidings run to great size. Thirteen are 12,000–14,000 feet long, six measure 9,000–11,000 feet, while only a few fit into a 8,000–9,000–foot category. Additionally, there are two "super sidings" where more than one train can fit. One is 19,163 feet, the other extends 24,081 feet. These extra long ones are referred to as "bonded, controlled sidings," meaning they have midpoint signal indication.

Marysville, Kansas, exemplifies today's midway terminal, really a yard where locals can work and where slower trains can be pulled aside to let the speedier moves run around. Rather than put a low-priority train out on the main ahead of a faster one, dispatchers often hold them at division points to reduce the number of meets.

With some 30 trains a day on the North Platte–Kansas City route, Marysville is a busy place. As each successive train rolls to a stop, brief conversation is exchanged about locomotive performance, along with a pleasantry or comment about the weather. Within moments, sometimes before brakeman and conductor are settled in a rear unit cab, wheels are rolling, acceleration building. The lead diesels are already approaching U.S. Highway 36, air horn in full cry. For 110 cars of solid coal, that interlude might be five minutes; on a stack train, under three. It also depends how many arrivals are piled up ahead or behind.

While this may be rural Kansas in appearance, it is freeway-style railroading.

A considerable amount of coal crosses the Marysville Subdivision to the southwest, generally via Missouri Pacific links. From Bailey Yard

Opposite: The Kansas City–North Platte line has been turned into a busy steel freeway as more and more coal business has been added. Here, in northern Kansas, an empty unit coal train is on the return trip portion of its journey.

3667
3667
3257

through Gibbon Junction, across alternating fields of corn and snow to Kansas City and beyond, the big SD60s ply their specialized assignments, running through the crowded big city terminal to the Van Buren and Missouri Divisions of onetime MoPac identity. The unit-train concept remains intact from mine to power plant and back. The only interruption is a service stop at North Platte's engine terminal.

From Marysville, the unsignaled Beatrice Branch drifts north through wheat country to Valley on the Nebraska Division. Before the merger with MoPac, this provided a roundabout routing between Omaha and Kansas City. Today UP uses the less circuitous ex-MoPac line between these two Missouri River cities. This line, known as the Falls City Subdivision, is part of the Kansas Division, and a mixed usage of CTC and ABS reflects its secondary mainline status.

As you pass through northeast Kansas along UP's route, numerous pieces of abandoned lines pop up. Small grain elevators, normally of early 1900s vintage, sit beside empty space; a nearby street crossing still clutches embedded pieces of rail. Not far away a dilapidated depot stands where telegraph keys pounded out their dit-dot-dit of another time frame. Some of these remnants belonged to UP, others from corporate charters of homespun fame.

Union Pacific was never a large branchline player on its eastern side. Its present network in northeast Kansas mainly stems from Missouri Pacific origins, with one principal exception: that slim, extended line taking off west of Topeka and crossing into Colorado as far as Denver. It seems to create an important link along the southern edge but in fact is viewed as a gatherer in wheat belt territory as well as a relief valve for the main trunk farther north. Typically a once-a-day through train in each direction is its stock in trade backed up by the usual quota of locals, turns or extras as needed in harvest time. On occasion, 100-car grain moves, even solid coal trains, traverse its 500-mile course, gradually ascending the great plains in eastern Colorado.

"Good track" is a routine comment about this line. Though relatively slow and mostly under TWC, it can handle the largest, heaviest trains that UP can dish out. Matter of fact, from Oakley, where the Kansas Division funnels into the Cheyenne Division, there is exactly one two-mile-long speed restriction in 255 miles, and that is for five miles less than the maximum. In other words, you can run at 40 mph for the Cheyenne Subdivision's entire length, Oakley to Denver. Not a bad average, at that.

True, its sidings are fundamentally short by modern standards—many are just either side of 3,000 feet—but grain trains, even unit-coal trains, are marked up for its full length, providing relief for the northern main line if it becomes exceptionally crowded.

With Bailey Yard the system's principal classifier, it makes sense that through trains, particularly merchandise traffic, will call there to be sorted. The southern route is not appealing for high-speed schedules, or for meets.

Marysville, Kansas, is crew change point between North Platte and Kansas City, a line that sees perhaps 25–30 trains a day at present. An eastbound is just starting to roll in this scene.

It provides its own traffic base and is an alternative for trains that aren't in need of work. A plodding grain train headed for Portland can be kept off mainline rails for several hundred miles by routing through northern Kansas and Denver.

Usually secondary lines such as this are restricted more by manpower than physical factors. Other than during seasonal peaks, a limited number of pool crews are available to man trains. Extra movements normally have to be planned well in advance to ensure enough conductors and engineers. At times a full complement of engines and cars may wait for hours before moving, moored in place while the inbound crew takes its mandatory rest.

Served mainly by connections with trains running east-west across Nebraska and Wyoming, Denver is important to the UP though it doesn't have its own long-distance flow. The roads' Condensed Service Plan, which details scheduled through train movements across principal regions, shows only four symbols with a prefix or suffix including Denver. And these are short ties to Cheyenne and North Platte. The Condensed Service Plan doesn't list unit grain trains or pure coal movements or, for that matter, locals; it does indicate only those scheduled items that run regularly.

The Greeley Subdivision extends north from the city, eventually connecting with the heavy-duty east-west highway at Borie, where Sherman Hill levels out. Trains to or from North Platte split off at La Salle to connect on the east at Julesburg, Colorado.

Beyond the countless ties binding Kansas City to North Platte and its systemwide outlets, the southern edge of Union Pacific is pretty much a land of low-keyed railroading. That certainly doesn't diminish its significance, for the Kansas wheat belt and Denver's burgeoning metropolis contribute their share to the annual resume of carloadings. It is just that timed progress is not quite the god that competition has forced upon the railroad elsewhere.

9310

CRISS-CROSS

WHAT NORTH PLATTE'S corpulent terminal is to systemwide classification, a rough triangle of activity west of Green River, Wyoming, is to train movement, for it provides entry to the other phase of Union Pacific, the single-tracked empire. Bounded loosely by Green River, Pocatello and Salt Lake City, this tremendously important entrepot of forged steel brings together all those diverse components that line the Pacific Coast—be it an APLA5, Friday's stack train off the dock district of New York and headed for Los Angeles, a Stockton–Council Bluffs train running as STUS, or a Seattle–North Platte drag (SENP).

Having climbed above the red sandstone cliffs that flank Green River's ever-congested terminal, a westbound through movement looks to its symbolism for guidance as Granger's identification sign sweeps into view.

An outsider sees a train, one just like another. A dispatcher checks his trainsheet and electronic map to see just what that mobile light on a flat wall panel might be. Is it CSPDZ, three 9100-class engines synchronized to the needs of a high-stepping van train on its way to Portland, or a like consist of equal "Z" status carded for Oakland's tightly packed waterfront? Both have been chasing each other's block signals for hundreds of miles, pausing at places like Rawlins to refuel, or Cheyenne to trade handlers, racing on to create a never-ending joust with time.

Coming hard upon Granger a choice looms: Which for Portland? Which for Salt Lake City? Beyond that yet another decision: Northern California or Southern?

A whirring power switch will decide, conforming to commands issued from Omaha, a good day's train ride in the distance. One of hundreds of control points wired or microwaved to this far-off master, CP847, also marked down as Granger, is a 40-mph switch turnout designed to settle matters. The approaching set of brightly hued containers heels to a curve and Pocatello, Idaho. Northwest bound it is!

Moments later, switch points reversed, ties flex beneath another set of boiling diesels, traction motors screaming in full voice. This one's flat out

Opposite: Yesterday, Oakland's bustling port scene, today a stiff pull past the towering rocks of Echo, Utah. By tomorrow this "Z" hustler will be slipping through the switches and yard tracks in Chicago.

for Salt Lake City, where another decision will be made, Los Angeles or Oakland. Again the symbols will dictate.

Just as everything beyond Omaha or Kansas City passes through yard limit markers imprinted Bailey Yard, so must movements concerned with UP's single-track empire criss-cross this triangular pattern, which is a bridge between eastern and western portions of the UP.

The area does originate its own key activity. Collectively this creates a very active operation at North Yard, Salt Lake City's principal marshalling center.

Not too far north is Riverdale, a modest-sized collection of yard tracks in Ogden whose glory days belong to yesteryear when Western Pacific was a separate image and the local Ogden Union Railway and Depot Company was an active partnership involving Rio Grande, SP and UP in its collective embrace. Today these ancient ties have been shattered with UP feeding most westbound traffic to the former WP, while Rio Grande and SP have become as one with an impact on former interchange arrangements.

That was yesteryear's tradition. Today's has quite a changed demeanor as the onetime burden of moving tonnage eastward through Echo and Weber Canyons to the plateaus of Wyoming is just one link in a chain, each as important as any other. The conqueror, as elsewhere, is horsepower.

That thousand miles of two-lane expressway beyond Omaha has intermittent sections of one-way and two-way running but only here in northern Utah will you discover left-hand operation in vogue. It came about to take advantage of gradient.

With scheduled freights, especially high-profile ones, rhythm plays a distinct role on various segments of a major railroad, and it seems the routine surge between Evanston and Ogden is nocturnal. The area is just about a day's running time away from UP's two principal California destinations.

As dusk arrives the spectator sport of train-watching places a covey of priority schedules from Los Angeles and Northern California on this district. The pace has certainly accelerated from prior years when any move, even one of modest tonnage, had need of an additional set of driving wheels. Now a set of units sufficient to master Cajon Pass or Feather River Canyon will have little concern about what Utah presents in barrier-like fashion.

Although cramped at times, on occasion squeezed through a narrow crevasse between pillars of red stone rocks as at Echo, UP's Salt Lake Subdivision between Ogden and the Wyoming state line is fundamentally a graceful achievement of the early surveyor's art. Twin bridges cross meanderings of the Weber River, and tunnels pierce rock which would have been far easier to sidestep.

Despite the often tough appearance and historical reputation, the roadbed is moderately fast in both directions, leastwise across lower can-

UP's roster is not noted for a large clutch of switchers, a sure sign of its dependence on long-distance trunkline work, as opposed to gathering large numbers of carloadings. This scene is at Ogden, Utah, now largely abandoned as an important transfer point between UP and Southern Pacific.

yons. The upper stretch above Echo is still slow going for climbers but otherwise mastered rather handily, a circumstance illustrated some years ago when the author had an unexpected opportunity to ride the cab of a streamliner between Evanston and Ogden.

Arriving in Evanston about a half hour behind its advertised time, train No. 101, the *City of San Francisco,* made a brief pause as scheduled. The delay was causing some trauma, as the hogger was literally jumping up and down in his straight-backed seat, fidgeting as with a bad case of hives. Alternating between a glance at his pocket watch and back along the train line, he kept muttering, "Let's go, let's go." Finally reacting to a waved arm and "highball," we were off and charging uphill toward Wahsatch [timetable spelling], where the downhill spur takes root. Playing every curve and every stretch of tangent to its utmost allowance, we raced toward Ogden through a picture postcard sunset, light reflecting off sandstone cliffs burnt more than their usual deep red by a low sun. Almost continuously it seemed that the well-worn timepiece was in one hand, while the other hand played the throttle detents with the learned skill of a master craftsman.

With one hour and 35 minutes carded for this section, perhaps Union Pacific had enough play built into the *City's* timecard, or perhaps a few speed limit boards were slightly expanded in this daily joust with time. Whatever the case, at 6:05 P.M. No. 101 was pulling through the butterfly sheds at Ogden Union Depot. We'd overcome a half hour's tardiness in 76 miles. No longer a picture of anxiety, the engineer fondly examined his trusty watch one last time, grinning modestly, almost self-consciously at his accomplishment. One couldn't help but reflect that this is railroading as it should be.

There are no more streamliners gliding through these canyons of northern Utah. In their stead have come railroading concepts that 30 years ago would have been considered table talk for questionable futurists.

The night at Echo is temporarily free of growling diesels. The fading day's light is a thin, pale line across the high ridges of Wasatch National Forest. Farther down where Weber Canyon splits away from suburban life, the opening stanza is but moments away.

It begins near Morgan siding, one of those centerpieces that extend from one end to the other of the thousand-mile highway, their flexibility established with a "Y" arrangement that plugs into either track at both ends.

A heavy breathing trio of GEs is heard approaching from Ogden, not lugging, mind you, but certainly working hard with one of those extra-long doublestack sets from a California port. This generation of prime movers is quieter than its predecessors, but through the walled canyons of this narrow defile they still create an audible sense of massiveness, power and ability expanded by a thousand echoes.

On some railroads the passage of a long container train would highlight a day's events . . . here in the canyon there will be several "such notable happenings." Twenty minutes have gone by since the last container car with its blinking red orb disappeared around a curve. Already, indications of a follow-on are present. A faint odor of burnt diesel still lingers when another headlight floats, seemingly disembodied, from Ogden's direction. Along comes a couple of high-numbered SD40s trailing a recently arrived SD60 while powering a solid piggybacker through the night. Relatively short in stature, lugging distinctive UPS trailers in its consist, this one is without exception of primary concern for all involved. Those rubber-tired UPS vans are always incorporated in the swiftest moves, so competitively demanding is this particular shipper.

Making a judgment call about relative velocities, the pigs will be riding herd on the containers at some point beyond the left-hand running sector. Then a dispatcher will probably cross the faster one over and around, although both are "elites" on a railroad where such designation is commonplace.

Coming next in this nightly congregation of important travelers is a westbound move of nearly 60 solid auto racks. Drifting downgrade, its trio of new units is barely audible, as attested to by decibel ratings on plaques mounted at the factory.

As night trudges along, UP provides over a half-dozen more trains in three hours, most conforming to profiles best described as important, including one pure cut of mechanical reefers from California hellbent for Midwestern and eastern produce markets. Freight of mixed parentage, boxcars, gons, flats, *et al.,* often avoid these hours if possible. Their time is programmed to avoid interference from any surge of fast trains on a subdivision. While that might be around midnight in Weber Canyon, it could be during daylight on Nebraska's eastern plains.

Reflecting what was loaded in Chicago yesterday evening, the racehorses are maintaining their dialogue with speed through Kearny, Grand Island and other sidings on the day watch, while a second trick dispatcher signs on to a similar covey of fast ones departing North Platte the opposite way. In due time Utah and Wyoming express their roles as well.

On the way east from Ogden, roadbed slices through a narrow passage of rocks, then emerges upon a spreading valley until the famous Devils Slide monument indicates another walled-in access to yet another spreading vista of farmland. It too will conclude at Echo under pillars of red sandstone as rails make an abrupt turn into an upthrusting channel which runs for about two dozen miles, its one percent lift taking rapid hold of a train's progress. Eventually, after a few tunnels and a criss-cross plan

High in the Wasatch Mountains in Rio Grande territory, a cooperative effort between UP–Rio Grande brings an IPPX coal train down the western slopes and a date with a power plant near Lynndyl, Utah.

Red over green signals greet this coal run as it moves off the Provo Subdivision and onto Lynndyl Subdivision iron in northern Utah.

that returns trains to the normalcy of right-hand running, the spreading openness of western Wyoming is encountered. In lieu of vertical walls of etched rock, the horizon becomes one of horizontal extensions, flat tables of plateau in endless row upon row, their edges dropping to form a maze of depressions through which the railroad hop-scotches.

By no means straight or level, steel must flex often, climbing and descending in intermittent fashion across most of Wyoming into Cheyenne. Clearing Echo Canyon at Wasatch involves an elevation of 6,800 feet which quickly descends a few hundred feet into onetime division point Evanston. Just as quickly it clambers up again to around 8,000 feet at the next apex, Altamont, 12 miles beyond. Picking up the course of Antelope Creek and then Muddy Creek beyond, rails drop back to 6,500 feet almost into Granger before taking one further slide into Green River and on *ad infinitum*. It is down one sag and up the next for boundless miles, topped off by that granddaddy of all, Sherman Hill.

If one ever wondered why this railroad favors turbocharged prime movers and the most horsepower that a builder could cram into successive generations, one need look no further than western Wyoming as justification.

Way off at the opposite end of this northern Utah district is the Provo Subdivision, which doesn't quite carry the accolades of a principal component, though it is a major player in the coal trade. It slips southeast out of Salt Lake City's North Yard, loops into Provo and then back again to the main line on the Escalante Desert near Lynndyl. Its basic priority lies south of Provo as evidenced by its application of CTC between that city and Lynndyl. What turns out to be a heavy dosage of annual tonnage is generated in partnership with the Rio Grande and shortline Utah Railway. UP has long had a working relationship with the latter, in past years providing it with leased diesel power while offering an outlet for its full-sized coal drags as they come smoking down the heavy grades. Pulled into the next-door UP yard at Provo, Utah Railway's loads go rolling south toward Los Angeles or to intermediate points by way of the Provo Sub, or perhaps to North Yard for other destinations.

Between Provo and Salt Lake's North Yard UP can move trains over its own rails or on Rio Grande's main line. Heavy moves prefer the foreign road steel that funnels past the Columbia-Geneva Steel Works, a destination for ore trains out of southern Utah around Cedar City or from as far away as the Mesabi Range in upper Minnesota.

While the Provo Sub's 135-mile extension may have a somewhat back road personality in the suburbs, south of Provo it reverts to basic Union Pacific heavy-duty-profile 133-pound steel, immaculately groomed roadbed and signal sets that can be tuned in electronically back there on the Missouri River's banks. It never was and is not now programmed for high speed, providing a comfortable 50-mile-an-hour territory extending between Provo and Lynndyl, a more than sufficient gait for the likes of solidly built coal trains which comprise its basic fare. A cooperatively owned generating station at Delta, Utah, burns plenty of coal from Carbon County—courtesy of Utah Railway-Rio Grande-Union Pacific engine crews. Then, too, much of the coal going to Southern California or to waiting ships in Los Angeles' harbor begins its trip under UP management at this point.

Coal could come out of the northern Utah mines by way of North Yard and then on to the south but by having the Provo Sub in place the trip is considerably shortened and far more efficient.

As for power, it's the contemporary standard of UP's coal-hauling brigade, principally SD60s in both traditional and blunt-nosed styling along with occasional fill-ins by the now elderly SD40s and sometimes

Off the coast at Oakland, an eastbound container rambles up Weber Canyon in December 1989.

newer Dash-8s. So there's nothing like a diminished capacity hereabouts, even though the Provo Sub is a bit off the beaten path.

Another optional course created by the steel-drawn chart in northern Utah is a link with the Northwest, one not exactly overwhelmed by traffic density yet not unimportant either. Listed as the Ogden Subdivision it ties together the area around Pocatello—and thus by extension the Northeast—with rail links beyond Salt Lake City to the south and west. Development has taken over north of Ogden toward Brigham City where many industries provide waybills for UP to process. There is also the through link between the railroad's extended segments along the Pacific Coast. Timewise this is not a route that caters to premier freight runs, given the fact that UP would be at a considerable disadvantage in attempting to compete along the Pacific Coast between north and south given the great inland sweep that it would have to travel. Where the clock is less of a consideration, UP does schedule freights between Hinkle and Los Angeles, but on a very relaxed schedule. This is also one of the few places where passenger trains still ply their trade. Amtraker Nos. 25 and 26 utilize the line to provide daily service between Salt Lake City and Portland, Oregon.

Perhaps this subdivision is best identified by its rather uncharacteristic—at least for Union Pacific—long-standing ties to an ABS system rather than a pushbutton personality.

Opposite: A bit long for the yard tracks at North Yard in Salt Lake City . . . a westbound APL train curves out of sight to the rear as it waits on a new crew before heading down the LA&SL to Southern California.

Taken collectively, northern Utah, with its connecting ties in all directions, is a transition, from double-tracked to single-tracked empires, from wherever Union Pacific comes from to wherever Union Pacific is going on the single-track portion of its western empire.

3463
3341
APL

Slipped into a siding north of Milford to meet a loaded coal train, a set of empty hoppers rolls out onto the main line again as it works its way back to the Midwest for grain loading.

An empty train of coal cars coming back from Los Angeles is seen running across the lower edge of the Provo Subdivision, heading back to Rio Grande interchange and a refill.

Opposite: The driving force on the lower half of the Provo Subdivision is coal and here, in 1990, the latest in UP motive power, a wide-nosed Dash-8, leads a coal train out of Provo Yard toward Southern California and a date with an oceangoing ship.

9380
9380
6118

9026
9026
MISSOURI PACIFIC
9026
UNION PACIFIC

FLAT OUT AND GREEN ...

IN A RECENT FINANCIAL newspaper column, a railroad official—not from UP—was quoted as saying that trains have an image of "slow and dumpy." Realistically, he couldn't be discussing the "Z" trains.

On Union Pacific, an attachment of the alphabet's last letter means a first-rate priority. In another era you appended obvious labels such as first class, second class, extra, even third class. Now when your entire far-flung empire is almost totally dominated by computer dispatching, how can you convey a feeling of urgency to certain schedules? Today's trains have in many instances become a rolling inventory for shippers, so competition and common sense dictate on-time performance with little tolerance for failure.

Perhaps 25–30 percent of the 700 or so trains on the system's daily trainsheet bear the suffix "Z." An OANPZ, for example, describes an Oakland–North Platte train of definite high priority. Essentially all trains today are scheduled, meaning that their performance, expected and actual, is monitored by the traffic control system. Some, however, do not distinguish between these terms, while their tightly crafted timetables represent the thoroughbreds in UP's stable.

They are treated accordingly as we shall see.

Los Angeles' East Yard is enveloped by a bit of early-morning dampness with dawn still an hour or so distant.

Somewhere around 4 A.M. the LACSZ (Los Angeles–Canal Street, Chicago) has been declared almost ready for its daily combat with a clock and almost 2,300 miles of thin steel.

Five A.M. comes and goes. Despite its carded rollout time, LACSZ is motionless under the sodium vapor lamps at East Yard. Those expected UPS trailers haven't come aboard yet, and while some shippers might be looking at empty space at this moment, one of the nation's largest waybill producers generates more respect.

Given a few moments of unexpected time, we can establish the vitals. Power is as presumed, heavyweight: a trio of Dash-8s, No. 9197 (lead) with the 9198 and 9201 trailing, a 12,000-hp assemblage. This physique is

Opposite: Off in the starkly bare desert canyons north of Las Vegas, Nevada, two big GE units of Missouri Pacific registry power an EB mixed COFC/TOFC train on a summer day in 1987.

not overpowering considering that two tough California barriers, Cajon Pass and Cima Hill, loom between downtown Los Angeles and Las Vegas.

Other essentials explained on the train's summary sheet indicate there are 43 loads, no empties, while Extra 9197 East, the trainsheet marking, will total 2,878 tons stretching over 3,799 feet. One five-car container set is included; otherwise this is a van train.

Well constructed to perform at maximum limits of 70 mph, LACSZ, at 15 minutes past the hour, is a bit anxious to get on with it.

"We're going," is said emphatically aboard locomotive 9197, and at 5:18 A.M. inertia becomes past tense as dozens of wheelsets turn ever so slightly. Since couplers are almost slackless on trains like these, the 12,000 hp just eases along and goes.

A rear brakeman on the second unit back had been complaining that the refrigerator wasn't on-line and substitute ice wasn't aboard. So the road foreman of engines, on hand for a check ride, exercised his prerogatives of command. Ice or no ice this train is on its way and if need be it can be grabbed at Yermo up the line.

While a brakeman is paid to work, a road foreman of engines must answer to a higher authority.

Traffic on the nearby Santa Ana Freeway is already building toward its morning commuter stalemate as No. 9197 leads slowly out of yard limit restraints. The engineer moves his throttle into Run One, while a voice over the cab radio says, "Have a safe trip."

The city is just waking, as acceleration soon sinks yard markers into oblivion. Now the 16-cylinder, turbocharged prime movers are showing their mettle, purring along with relative ease as Whittier Junction looms ahead. Here Southern Pacific ties in with its harbor area tonnage, utilizing UP iron for a half-dozen miles before veering away to its own City of Industry yard nearby. Some mornings an Espee stacker will be waiting for UP to clear, but not this particular day.

Flashing lights at street crossings, persistent blasts from an overhead air horn warn motorists on the 50-mile course to West Riverside. Top speed will be 60 in these suburbs.

The Los Angeles Subdivision claims territorial jurisdiction over 163.7 miles, of which 102.1 belong to Santa Fe. The latter serves as host between West Riverside and Daggett in the Mojave desert.

Beyond a stone bridge just before West Riverside, a signal displays a flashing yellow indication, noted by a slight nudge of the air-brake handle. "Approach Limited" is its message, a restrictive 40 mph that sets the stage for a smooth fusing into Santa Fe's fast-paced double track to San Bernardino and the ladder of Cajon Pass.

Momentarily, AT&SF double track looms around a curve where another signal with red over flashing green offers a "Diverging Clear Limited" indication, allowing LACSZ to enter a dual-control switch turnout at 40 mph. Not too many years ago that gateway to trackage rights would have been restrained to a jogging 15 mph, but some track realignment and a high-speed turnout have easily saved 20 minutes per train.

Of such ongoing, often costly but minor improvements, are high-speed schedules made. And met!

Barely into its long journey, LACSZ has an ambitious goal to meet. With 12,000 hp and just under 3,000 tons of girth it meets the optimum horsepower per total ton standard, calculated at 4:1, between Los Angeles and western Nebraska. Beyond North Platte, that ratio drops to a factor of three, so a unit may be shed before moving further. Power is never wasted on UP.

The schedule calls for a 0500 departure out of Los Angeles on Day 1; Salt Lake City, 0230 Day 2; Cheyenne, 1550 Day 2; North Platte, 2120 Day 2; Fremont, 0320 Day 3; with Chicago's Canal Street marking the trip's finish at 1615 on Day 3. Allowing for time zone differentials, that's an average of roughly 40 mph start to stop. Included in that picture is an allocation of 175 minutes for switching, crew changing and fueling. As an

Early morning finds the LACSZ run hugging the main line in Santa Fe territory as a westbound freight comes through the yard at San Bernardino after having dropped off some interchange traffic.

An eastbound trainload of mostly empties has just topped Cajon Pass, and is still hugging the left-hand side of Santa Fe's Cajon Subdivision iron as it gathers speed to cross the high desert.

example, 40 minutes are set aside at Las Vegas, 45 at Salt Lake City, and 30 at Cheyenne. In that time a train can be switched, have fuel added, or be given a 1,000-mile inspection.

Meantime, back at West Riverside, the engineer eases back on a throttle; when he calculates that the last cars have straightened out, he pushes ahead on his power setting.

From the outside, Santa Fe's Riverside–San Bernardino section appears as cut-up, patchy blocks of land alternating between housing tracts and light industry. From a cab it's a wide highway given to intermittent stabs of colored light. Opposing train movements drift by on their own lane, swirling dust before fading away to a fleeting memory.

The event is deceptively relaxing. Whether a 3,000-ton lightweight or 10,000 tons of rolling grain, the physics are daunting. No stopping here on a proverbial dime. Running room to the next signal and beyond is always uppermost in one's mind.

Approaching Santa Fe's San Bernardino Yard, velocity is trimmed, as the first UP through freight is seen, a Yermo–Los Angeles drag dropping cars. After a few tight curves through town, the 16 cylinders behind a bulkhead now start to lug a mite, sounding louder than they did a few minutes ago, as the initial tug of Cajon Pass is felt.

Cajon is no longer the barrier it used to be, especially to light TOFC/COFC moves, but the challenge is still there, though mostly in terms of time. LACSZ merely settles down to a steady 25-mph gait and holds. Unless something unexpected or untoward happens, an engineer figures 45–50 minutes on the hill to Summit, a forecast rarely wrong. Tonnage trains on both UP and Santa Fe still rate helpers, although UP will employ a through helper all the way to Milford, Utah, on a long stack train going to North Platte.

Since there's nothing close ahead, LACSZ is expecting a smooth, steady assault on the 2.2 percent grade of the pass.

Near Verdemont, a trio of Espee tunnel motors pulls alongside and ahead of UP's piggybacker. Moving faster, those red and grey units trail covered hoppers, and after less than two-dozen car lengths comes a caboose, the whole not much of a chore for a three-motor lashup. A good-natured blast of an airhorn brings a like response from up ahead.

When Cajon Pass was restructured some years ago, two-way signaling was installed so that the traditionally separate eastbound and westbound lines were made bi-directional. Now you're likely to see lithe piggybacks climbing the former 3.0 percent descending track.

At this moment, UP's "Z" is coming upon Sullivan's Curve, that famous icon of railroad real estate where two paths go their separate ways to Summit. If there was a question as to which trail might be followed, it's settled by tonnage, for only real lightweights of 2,200 tons or less and short of 3,000 feet extension are accorded a privilege of going up the down staircase.

Topping out at Summit's reconstructed scene, sustained momentum is swiftly regained, entering several miles of long, flowing curves which split the high desert towards Victorville. Deceptively though, for westbounds encounter 1.60 percent here all the way to Summit, enough, in fact, for UP to station a couple of two-unit helper sets at Victorville for Cajon Pass duty. One is already at work for as we duck under a laboring train at Frost two yellow SD40s are pumping hard on the bunched slack of a train heading for Summit. Before resignaling, this section of Santa Fe exhibited left-hand running and it was here at Frost that an overpass had twisted directions or righted them depending upon direction. Now it doesn't matter for either rail in either direction is the setup soon to be illustrated at Victorville, just the other side of the Mojave Narrows, as our van train is channeled through a crossover and down the left-hand side. Reasoning is soon apparent as just past town a long coal train with UP–Rio Grande power is fouling the right-hand main, pulling into a cement plant where the Mojave Northern Railroad, a local short line, is headquartered.

Two signal bridges beyond and it's back to the right-hand main, just in time to let two Santa Fe piggybackers by for Los Angeles. After a few restricted curves, the line opens to speed, and unless overtaking another train—a doubtful proposition—a clear road into Barstow and beyond is assured.

Bypassing Santa Fe's huge Barstow terminal on a high-speed through track, LACSZ continues nine miles to Daggett and a junction that brings it back to home iron. From now on the next several hundred miles over the old Los Angeles and Salt Lake trail will feature single-track railroading. Now that it's back on UP the "Z" brand will accord this train a deferential position unless it comes upon equals and then closeness to a siding will probably determine which blinks first.

Yermo! The high desert's yard is so close to Daggett that no attempt at regaining a high-speed posture will be made. Until a few years back Yermo was just a sleepy desert community, owing its existence to a Spanish-style stucco depot and the UP crews which traded mounts there. With Los Angeles' East Yard being pushed to its limits the railroad opted to redo Yermo, extending its size and assigning industrial blocking chores for Southern California industries. Quite a few trains are now worked at Yermo in contrast to past times when its sole function was to mark up crews for Las Vegas or Los Angeles.

Eschewing Yermo, today's high-stepper drifts on through, the brakeman who complained about ice in East Yard apparently now mollified. Two tracks extend east of town for five miles, plenty of room to adjust opposites meeting one another on this lower edge of the Cima Subdivision. Matter of fact, there's a hard yellow block showing already—Rule 245C, Approach Medium at no more than 30 mph—making itself known. Since it's about 10 A.M., the source is well known: Amtrak No. 35 from Salt Lake City. As it passes down the right-hand side, the turnout signal ahead flashes Rule 245A, "Proceed," green over red. Immediately there is a surge in power, for the turnout here at Toomey is good for 40 mph. No sense in wasting time!

Less than 20 minutes later the rocky beauty of Afton Canyon is apparent. Reds, oranges and yellow dye the steep-sided cliffs as rails explore their way through this rocky defile. Long-framed trailer flats screech a bit in protest as flanges press against outer rail.

Relatively brief in linear terms, Afton is followed by the real desert: shifting sand and sagebrush as far as can be seen. The pace quickens, then suddenly a flashing yellow appears where none should be. An engineer in CTC territory rarely knows what's ahead, depending totally upon a dispatcher's manipulation of buttons for guidance. If a signal says siding, then siding it is; if it confers main line, then that is right, too.

When there shouldn't be any opposing symbols of high priority nearby, the idea of having yellow thrown in your face is a mite surprising, even unsettling.

A late afternoon in November 1988 finds a three-unit set just about topping the hill at Cima, California, with a long string of empty covered hoppers in tow. Helpers in this area are a rare exception, although some of the heavy stack trains will have through helpers between Los Angeles and Milford, Utah.

The next signal is a fixed yellow, then comes red over green where Crucero Siding swings away to the left. Way down toward the opposite end of its 5,765-foot length, an opposing train is just hoving into view, headlight centered in a dark spot beneath a vertical sun. A snort of disgust escapes the road foreman of engines as he briskly reaches for an ever handy notebook. Later today, maybe tomorrow, a dispatcher on duty will be called to a company phone . . . why?

It's not supposed to be this way. This was not an encounter of equals. A commoner ahead of a prince? Protocol has been abused.

Impatiently under way again, LACSZ lithely skips across the barren surface, its agility readily apparent as it snakes through a switch and out on the main in a wink. Coming upon Kelso another yellow is observed, but not with frustration for now Cima Hill is in sight while the troika of huge GEs will do well to maintain a steady 25 mph on this desert ladder. Open-faced, circuitous to a mild degree, Cima Hill used to be a helper district till diesels came along. The only additional power it experiences these days is on extra-heavy stack trains, those 28 well car (five regular cars counted as one) sets which run all the way from Los Angeles to Milford, Utah, with a couple of SD40s bringing up the rear as through helpers.

A few thousand yards ahead and two sidings above, the yellow signal's rationale is quite apparent, for another movement is well into its climb and easily spotted on this barren patch of sagebrush and sand.

This is one place on Union Pacific where "retainer use" is not some arcane tradition from the past. Heavy westbound trains, especially grain and coal, are often obliged to stop at Cima. Lighter ones can generally bypass the need but any train exceeding 80 tons per operative brake must come to a halt at Cima to turn up retainers. The only out is if there are two horsepower effective dynamic brake per trailing ton. Logically, then, a 10,000– 12,000-ton freight would need more units than commonly assigned to ignore that standard. Descent of Cima Hill is usually a time-consuming adventure for heavyweights and under certain circumstances the ritual calls for a 10-minute, wheel-cooling stop at Dawes, halfway along.

Cima Hill finds our "Z" gradually gaining on its companion ahead. Signals are geared for the terrain, so we can trail along a little closer than would be prudent in higher speed territory. That option, which allows many trains to continue without stopping is always a desirable prospect on a heavy grade.

Expectations notwithstanding, a dispatcher allows the preceding move to hold mainline steel all the way to Cima where it heads into one of two sidings. The other is already plugged by a westbound, a solid coal train of mostly Rio Grande hoppers from northern Utah. It's easier for both these holed-up moves to leave at the grade's crest—the westbound trail rises, too, at the summit—rather than struggle forth from hillside locales.

"Yes sir, you had a good roll-by," spits forth from the cab radio on lead unit No. 9197, as one of the passed trains falls away behind.

While westbounds pull a slow march up from a dry lakebed along the Nevada–California state line, there is no such restriction on the descending grade. It is open country and fast. Roadbed falls away from Cima through a small forest of low-lying Joshua trees. The speed needle now hovers at "70 per," and somehow those twin ribbons which provide guidance look awfully slim considering 200-ton locomotives and almost 3,000 tons of train. Ivanpah, then Moore sidings fly by in rapid-fire order while at Nipton a westbound van train is comfortably tucked in well ahead of our arrival. It does not mar the steady stream of green boards which have accompanied this train beyond Cima's lofty perch.

As expectations have been ratcheted upwards toward "Run 8" and held there, the ever-present notebook sits unmarked in the road foreman's shirt pocket. Things are as they should be now.

A long downward spiral awaits this set of SD40s as they begin the downward path from Cima to Kelso, California, in the Mojave Desert.

Given the clarity of vision on this portion of the Mojave Desert and the elevated path that UP takes, a stationary observer can often follow a train for half an hour or more.

Skipping along the fringe of a dusty, sun-bleached dry lake, UP marks its entry into Nevada. The end of lap one for LACSZ is now in the offing. First, however, comes a real slowdown, a wide, extended U-curve at Sloan to be followed by a few miles of heavily contorted running through the hills that lead to Las Vegas. Emerging into the southern suburbs of Nevada's famous gambling city, a cautious pace will be maintained as numerous street crossings echo to a familiar ding-ding-ding of warning bells.

At 1403 hours, the glittery impressions of Las Vegas casinos appear off to the right as LACSZ lurches slightly on its way to a yard track. The conductor drops off at the yard office to inform St. Louis' National Car Center that indeed his charges have arrived as expected. A few minutes of scheduled leeway in town allow for exchange—two cars dropped off, three added. With two westbounds already poised and ready to roll, it was easier to shove the piggybacker through track No. 13. Otherwise, it would have stayed aboard high iron.

Beyond Nevada there will be working time allocated at Salt Lake City, Cheyenne and North Platte plus 15 minutes for a mainline refueling at Rawlins. Apart from that, only five-minute crew changes are programmed and often they are accomplished in less time.

This is the way of the "Z," a mark of something special.

NORTH OF LAS VEGAS

IT HAS BEEN Union Pacific for decades, but the line southwest out of Salt Lake City is still popularly referred to as "the LA&SL" after the previous owner, the Los Angeles and Salt Lake Railroad. Those initials identify the purest example of solitary desert railroading in western America, even more so than sections of ex-Western Pacific iron. The line certainly spans a vaster territorial expanse, for barring a few sections of suburbia at either terminus and the neon-tinged oasis in Las Vegas, the single-track route pretty much shuns population clusters. Taking a reasonable direct course across what geologists call the basin and range province for its intermittent mountains and valleys, LA&SL exists in an essentially arid atmosphere with landforms to match.

Though the northern portion exhibits extensive patches of roadbed that permit the railroad's "70-per" jogging style to be practiced, its midriff and southern reaches are, on average, among UP's slowest subdivisions.

The Utah Division, stretching from Salt Lake City to Las Vegas, is organized into two subdivisions: the Lynndyl Sub, 206.8 miles between Salt Lake City and Milford; and the 242.5-mile Caliente Subdivision, Milford to Las Vegas. At that point, California Division jurisdiction begins. This division also has two main components: the 171.2-mile Cima Sub between Las Vegas and Yermo; and the Los Angeles Sub between Yermo and Los Angeles. Nearly 60 percent of the Los Angeles Sub's 163.7 mainline miles are on Santa Fe iron, the result of a 1905 trackage rights agreement.

Of the three principal carriers that enter Southern California, Union Pacific's Los Angeles investment is the slimmest in relative terms. This is not to denigrate its size or performance, for by any measure the operation fits a lifestyle of high-class action, detailing 20–24 full-sized trains every 24 hours. Most circulate by way of Los Angeles' East Yard, while a few—generally unit trains of coal or grain—head on through toward the ever-growing harbor district. That, by anybody's measure, is heavy-duty railroading. The Union Pacific's traffic levels from Southern California are surprisingly good considering the fact that it is not served by a network of

Opposite: Early morning finds yesterday evening's stack train out of Los Angeles working through the steep-walled canyons of Meadow Valley Wash in southern Nevada. The train is well on its way toward joining the chorus of hotshots on the Great Steel Turnpike.

UNION PACIFIC
6062

Long before the era of Japanese imports and TV, this old store building on the Utah–Nevada border was pumping gas into "39" Fords and Chevies. Now the store is abandoned and diesels roll by instead of high-wheeled mallets.

radiating lines on the regional scale of SP or Santa Fe.

Elsewhere, we've chronicled the high adrenalin workings of an "LACSZ" between the local container yard in Los Angeles and Nevada's southernmost gambling city, including some of the physical features encountered en route. So now we'll zero in on what lies north of Las Vegas, or if you prefer to encounter it by timetable direction, to the east as the dispatcher calls out.

Las Vegas, like Milford further up the line or Yermo to the south, is a popular place to make meets between trains, especially since less time-urgent moves can be briefly shunted aside while a freight forwarder set or stack train cruises on by. Many drags and unit style bulk haulers have sit-and-wait time sculpted into their routine. So while a "Z's" crew is called to high energy service, others cool their flanges for a while, perhaps eschewing a meet further along, holding back till the hot ones have cleared town.

Stationary consists in Las Vegas don't imply that UP isn't in command of its destiny. Often they are taking on fuel from a mainline stanchion while they're waiting to be passed. When slack was stretched out of Los Angeles or Salt Lake City, almost 100 percent odds said that such down time was optioned in Vegas. Union Pacific can't conceive of running its system any other way.

Penetrating a series of elongated trenches that begins at Moapa, 50 miles north of Las Vegas, the railroad shares its roadbed with rattlesnakes, coyotes, and little else as it enters the Meadow Valley Wash. Raw-looking vertical cliffs display varicolored rock whose countenance changes with every hour as the sun's stare shifts, creating shadowy portraits in tableau.

Moapa stands at the southern portal of the wash, 118 miles of flange-squealing, train-bending, often hard-climbing railroad in the inimitable style of the modern-day Union Pacific, meaning the last ounce of perfor-

Opposite: About 30 miles north of Las Vegas, a freight speeds across the early morning desert toward Milford and Salt Lake City.

mance will routinely be squeezed from its frequently rugged and challenging profile.

Sophisticated roadbed, the latest in rolling stock and a mindset that appreciates how to make it mesh have combined to tame Meadow Valley Wash. Not many years ago, crews punched the clock between Milford–Caliente and Caliente–Las Vegas on separate shifts in the traditional slow motion of yesteryear. Currently, five- to six-hour assignments, Milford to Las Vegas, are routine. Watching aluminum trailers and rocking auto racks heel to a series of curves or slip between weathered blocks of sandstone illustrates how two words, contemporary and competition, are defined in the 1990s.

Meadow Valley Wash illustrates nature as a chain of beads, a back-to-back hookup of constricted alleys joined to one another by needle-eye gateways. Stretched out over this meandering section of railroad, a hefty-sized stack train could be strung out across a half-dozen curves at once, given train lengths that run to 8,000 feet or thereabouts. On an average, roughly every third or fourth siding across the entire LA&SL offers enough space for such participants, though it's expected they will have little need unless chancing upon an opposing clan member. Everyone else is considered an inferior contestant.

One can only marvel at the early planners who hacked their way across the expansive desert skyline on horseback, creating a steel causeway with basic plotting tools. There always seems to be a blank wall every few miles, but somehow a way was found by following the tiny stream from which the area derives its name.

By comparison, even Feather River Canyon seems a wide path alongside the meager space through which trains funnel in this desert rivulet.

Despite wresting every shred of momentum it can, UP's Meadow Valley Wash is not a place where the railroad expects to make much time on its long-distance scheduling. Thirty-mph speed boards are a fairly constant companion, eastbounds encountering one of the longest sustained climbs on the system, 78.5 miles of 1.5 percent or better from Carp Siding to suggestively named Crestline near the Nevada–Utah state line. Moapa rests at 1,671 feet; 110 miles later, Crestline looms large in a diesel's windshield at 5,992 feet altitude. In between, there is rarely any moment where trains are not hemmed in by an extended stadium of sagebrush and sandstone.

Starting from the south end at Farrier siding, MP 393—the next siding north of Moapa—extending to Uvada, MP 501.1, the absolute top velocity allowed is 50 mph, an exceedingly rare event. The list of speed restrictions is as detailed as a government manual, comprising four dozen between the mileposts listed above. The majority fall between 30 and 40 mph, with one or two tagged as low as 20 mph. Yet a spirited stack train making a determined assault on this rugged territory is every bit as progressive as UP hotshots elsewhere, although not so speedy. Simply put,

In Meadow Valley Wash near Caliente, a five-unit set of the latest power pulls a long container train toward Southern California.

there are physical limits, even these days, as to just how much money and determination can accomplish.

Thus, much of LA&SL's steel highway remains a crooked trail with one major alteration, an early 1980s' line change along the Utah–Nevada border that best illustrates how rescuing minutes becomes necessary to vie with your rivals.

From the north, UP races off the Escalante Desert, running into a mountain blockade every bit the equal of Sherman Hill in effort if not in fame. Just as Utah abuts Nevada, the Cedar Range, one of innumerable rises, stands firm. Nearby Caliente was one of UP's greatest helper terminals during steam; up to four engines were often needed to assist road power south of town and up the slopes to Crestline. From the north end, a short district was carved out to boost the heavier westbounds as well.

As with Wyoming's big hill, the local barrier was mastered by a line change and diesel power. Steam engines were the first to go, as thirstless diesels had completely taken over difficult desert terrain following World War II. The line change isn't all that elderly, dating from 1982 when an especially restrictive set of curves was eliminated and the line shortened by one mile through a project known as the Crestline Line Change. Just a year prior, Yermo's new classification yard had been stamped "finished," LA&SL's newly upgraded facilities falling into place just as a surge in traffic into and out of Southern California traffic emerged.

The old track contained 10 curves in seven miles, some up to 10 degrees in arc. The new alignment contains maximum one-degree, 25-minute curvatures plus an 8,800-foot siding, allowing a 50-mph entrance as trains race in from the north.

Acoustically, passage is dominated by screeching wheelsets, surging, noisy trainlines and, presently, softer expressions from grunting diesels.

Overall, the portion of UP's Los Angeles and Salt Lake Railroad between the border with Utah and Las Vegas is one of the slowest mainline sections the railroad owns. This scene is typical of why.

Although the current SD60s and Dash-8s have been well muted in terms of decibels, the still raucous utterances of SD40s are persistent, their turbocharged 16 cylinders vocally reminiscent of a generation that won't let go.

Los Angeles-bound trains stage west from the Utah–Nevada line into the chanting, high-pitched song of dynamic brakes on the way down toward Caliente. Coal trains typically go a step further, filling the desert air with the sounds of hard brake applications and the smell of warm, acrid brake smoke. Sometimes the drama is reinforced by an uncommon need for retarders. It's railroading in a hundred-mile hall of echoes.

Just south of Caliente a few extra-wide tunnels pierce hard granite, half occupied by single track, remnants of a time long ago when double tracking the wash was contemplated. It never materialized, so they exist as a monument to unfulfilled ambition of times past. Yet given today's LA&SL volume and the growth of Southern California, the railroad probably wishes such dreams had become three-dimensional reality.

Consider.

The port area of Los Angeles–Long Beach recently surpassed New York City in terms of annual tonnage potential, a measure of how UP's Salt Lake City–Los Angeles route is flourishing.

Spasms of train-sheet detail which afflict Nampa, Cheyenne, North Platte, even the corn fields of Kansas, are no stranger to Utah–California

Division dispatchers. At times, three, four, even five trains are rumbling along in succession, spaced by one or two sidings at best, to be followed by hours so hushed that only the loud crack of expanding rails or the beating of birds' wings shatters tranquility.

South of Caliente, eastbound trains feast upon an almost unbelievable few hundred yards of tangency, basically a teaser, for hardly have units been notched into a higher throttle position when they're back on the air again as bluffs crowd close, momentum settling into that measured cadence of a steady mountain grade.

Beyond Crestline's tree-laced summit, a northern vestibule opens up to allow the Union Pacific to do what it does so well, run high-speed symbols. Immediately there are a few miles of restraining performance as tonnage must be held back, but soon those beckoning speed boards with their double-digit "70s" have reappeared, all in a row, *ad infinitum.*

The Escalante is a different mode of desert than that tortured surface now left behind. It's an elongated valley, quite wide at times and in contemporary UP jargon, a mecca for the likes of the "Zs."

Those super engines, the pride of EMD and GE, really get to hum along at a fine, mileage-swallowing pace on the Escalante's expansive stage.

Oh sure, an intermittent mile or so of low-value climb still finds its way into LA&SL's cross-section, a minor affair to be sure in an otherwise conceptual view that conforms to an urban dweller's meaning of "desert."

Free of bondage, unrestrained by curvature or vertical gestures, the electronic/diesel partnership of third-generation locomotives rolls along

At one time, UP entertained the idea of double tracking its Meadow Valley Wash line below Caliente, Nevada, and even went so far as to double track (in width) a few tunnels. These extra-wide tunnels still stand as a monument to that unfulfilled promise.

Utah's Escalante at full gallop. Wind whips past the blunt nose of the lead unit, funnels rearwards around its slim engine housing, making it difficult to walk between units. Tightly buttoned up in the second unit, a brakeman has scant intention of coming forward unless absolutely necessary and then logically only when the pace has moderated.

Sidings, gapped eight to 10 miles apart, drift by relentlessly, cued at each approach by double signal lights, "green over red" beams displayed at the command of a computer hundreds of miles distant. A system hardly considered unique where "state-of-the-art" is an everyday expression.

Ever present, but mute, cab signals are not employed on Union Pacific's single-track empire, only on the throbbing steel turnpike with its double-wide roadbed between Omaha and Salt Lake City. So the first indication a hogger gets of siding time is usually a "yellow" well in advance of the next siding. While radio is obviously available, trains get their official instructions from wayside signals since a dispatcher can program in meets well in advance and then go on to other matters. Unless, of course, individual attention is needed and on these occasions radioed details are relayed in advance.

For instance . . .

Picture yourself privy to a conversation between Extra 6246 East and a Utah Division DS.

The extra is a coal empty out of Milford where crews are changed on all trains. Having sped across the desert to Lynndyl, it's engaged in local switching duties at the junction with the Provo Sub, a path it's headed for. Extra 6246 East brings together three big six-axled units and close to 90 empty hoppers, most of which are still coupled together as it switches cars to a few tracks alongside the main. There is a lot of banging and clattering going on as slack bunches and runs out with each move.

After 20 minutes or so of this behavior, some of which spills out on the main track, a rather irritated dispatcher comes on the radio. A westbound drag has come into Lynndyl's north siding and to the south a "Z"-marked symbol stands motionless before a brilliant red lens. "Stop and stay stopped," it dictates, not exactly as had been planned.

"Extra 6246 East, Lynndyl Sub dispatcher," is broadcast in tones a bit edgy.

"This is Extra 6246 East," comes a reply.

"You realize you've been holding up a stack train for over 15 minutes?"

In a flat tone, hardly displaying emotion, some voice from a super engine cab responds, "Well, you gave us a 90-car train and told us to switch Lynndyl, and the only way we can do it is to use the main."

A bit of resignation in his voice, the DS adds, "O.K., but hurry it up, that stack has to get moving."

That is individual attention and why there's still a human element in railroading, not just pre-digested software.

Late on a summer day, a "Z" train carves up the desert terrain of UP's Los Angeles and Salt Lake district. Sixty miles from its destination in Salt Lake City, the train has been burning up desert mileposts hour upon hour.

Beyond Lynndyl's junction the routes split, the Provo Sub which goes to the city of Provo where the UP picks up the coal tonnage that the Rio Grande and the Utah Railway bring across the Wasatch Range from the Carbon County mines. Meantime, the bulk of traffic keeps to a northward direction, skirting the lower edge of the Great Salt Lake, taking up a parallel course with what used to be the Western Pacific and then finding the width of North Yard waiting to embrace it.

Beyond North Yard, most trains will enter a totally new running style, the cab-signaled, double-tracked kingdom that splits the mesas of Wyoming and the windswept plains of Nebraska. A few will be split into segments, the bits and pieces programmed into a dozen different symbols with equally diverse destinies.

So goes the Los Angeles and Salt Lake Railroad of yesteryear, the Union Pacific Railroad of today.

APL
9169 9169
9167 9167

FROM ONE PACIFIC TO ANOTHER

SILENCE GRIPS THE desert for dozens of barren mileposts. Scattered dust devils dance momentarily with an afternoon breeze, then dissipate in the growing redness of a late afternoon Nevada sun. In the distance a piggybacker slips through the restraining clutches of a yard limit board at Winnemucca while farther west, an opposing movement has just traversed the restrictive, curving watercourse of Feather River Canyon. Accelerating to more open landscape, it emerges upon an arid, bleached landscape which will serve as its stage for many hours.

Somewhere in that time ahead, these two trains will meet in a darkened amphitheater. One will take the siding, the other the main.

As this brief encounter ends, Nevada's space will return to its normal quietude, and dazzling headlights will continue on to Salt Lake City and Oakland's bustling waterfront.

Beyond Union Pacific's operating department, arcane siding names like Jungo, Reynard or Cholona mean absolutely nothing. To railroaders who keep things humming on this onetime Western Pacific main, they are all important, the only places where conflicting moves can be accommodated.

UP puts in at every major ocean transfer point from Los Angeles to Seattle, a claim that no competitor, not Espee, Santa Fe, nor Burlington Northern, can make. As trade with the Pacific Rim grows, those yellow diesels are well positioned to handle a major share.

Evidence of these vibrant links are found far inland as well. Certainly the onetime "Wobbly," as WP was affectionately labeled before its acquisition by UP, helped that position become more intense. UP knew there was more to the Western Pacific than the renowned Feather River Canyon.

If sheer drawbar pull could reduce the status of Feather River to routine subdivision, UP would have easily made a change. But the Dash 8s which tear up western Nebraska at 70 per or the SD60s which single-handedly move a 110-car coal train across the North Platte Sub are incapable of negotiating more than a snail's pace across the wye-shaped bridge at Keddie or the 360-degree motion on Williams Loop. Regardless

Opposite: An eastbound pig train is powered by an all-GE trio including two Dash-8s and a U30C as it heads up the Feather River Canyon toward Portola, California, in 1988.

of future developments, Feather River Canyon will retain its reputation as a slow, tortuous place to run trains. Gradient is of little matter either, though the average climb is a constant one percent. Trains in either direction take roughly four hours to cover the winding, tunnel-strewn course from Oroville to Portola. Today the route is considerably more active than it was. Unit trains of coiled steel, extended-length stack trains and manifest freights are routine fare.

Yet before we express greater interest in Feather River Canyon's railroad showmanship let's turn to a less illuminated phase of today's line into Northern California, the segment hinged to Salt Lake City's North Yard.

Like the Mojave Desert or portions of the old Los Angeles and Salt Lake Railroad down the Escalante Valley toward Las Vegas, UP's westward run on ex-WP steel offers unique vistas of endless depth. Few locales can provide this measure, where a train at speed can remain in sight for 20–30 minutes from a stationary spot. (And if it is a solid coal or grain train whose motion is restricted, an even longer viewing time is guaranteed.)

Hundred-mile-long combinations of mountain, high plateau and unpatterned topographic features proliferate to a greater degree than just about anywhere else on the UP.

When Western Pacific was able to project itself east of the Rockies with D&RGW cooperation, the marketing combination never offered the efficiency of a single carrier, a dimension that UP created through its purchase of WP.

The truth is that 922 miles of basically single track from Salt Lake City to Oakland would be far busier and profitable as a two-division slice of UP than it could be as a struggling independent with connections. The onetime autonomy of Western Pacific never quite created enough funds to meet modern-day competition head-on. There were days—all too often—when perhaps only two or three through trains plied the lonely desert across northern Nevada in a manner all too reminiscent of Milwaukee Road's abandoned trail to the Northwest.

Former Western Pacific trackage is a two-divisional scheme under UP's tutelage. Departing from the Utah Division's course toward Southern California at a connection called Smelter—in obvious deference to a nearby copper plant—the Nevada Division covers part of Utah and all of northern Nevada, leaving off at Portola just as the famous canyon leading into central California is encountered. At that point the aptly named Feather River Division breaks trail, flowing across the Central Valley and coastal mountains to eventually terminate at San Francisco Bay. The twin divisions encompass compatible mileage: 675 for the Feather River, 841 for the Nevada. While there is a fair amount of branchline territory included in the former's outline, the latter is fundamentally mainline action, save for a couple of short extensions on the east end and the Reno Branch on its other. Otherwise, it is pure running territory.

Approaching a 40-mph turnout at Smelter, movements bound for the

Having crossed over the climb at Silver Zone Pass in eastern Nevada, a Stockton-bound train now races across a low valley near Shafter where, at one time, connections were made with the Nevada Northern Railway.

Nevada Division slip onto Lake Subdivision iron and initiate a gradual turn from southwest to west along the rim of the Great Salt Lake. Like Espee to the north with the Lucin cut-off, UP has been forced to elevate its roadbed along dozens of miles of embankment to keep rising waters at bay. Just past the lake, tracks cut through the dazzling-white surface of Bonneville Salt Flats till the Nevada state line is crossed at Wendover.

Appearances abruptly change. Now steel enters the basin and range province, a self-descriptive term from the pages of a geology textbook, the look which will prevail until the great Sierra Nevada roadblock is encountered. Near Wendover is Silver Zone Pass, a slow climb containing one radical, U-shaped curve. From there, roadbed sets off south and finds a low level crossing of the Pequop Mountains, through a long tunnel at 5,700 feet. This is the way Western Pacific did it. This is the way its successor does, too.

Turning north again, UP meets the rails of Southern Pacific at Wells, Nevada. Rivals though they may be, the two railroads display a spirit of cooperation in the center of Nevada. Between Alazon—four miles from Wells—and a connection just short of Winnemucca, 168 miles west, the two carriers run railroad lines within a few hundred yards from each other. Southern Pacific is designated to carry all westbound traffic; UP handles

The long shadows of late afternoon extend through Palisades Canyon near Carlin, Nevada, as a fast westbound heads for the Pacific Coast with a piggyback train.

eastbound assignments. Their respective signal systems are set accordingly, with Rule 251 in effect on UP.

Crossovers exist at Carlin (SP crew change point) and Elko (ditto for UP) as a convenience so that each road's trains can get back on home territory momentarily. Otherwise the two companies run a joint facility, an essentially ABS-controlled duo of tracks across the heartland of northern Nevada.

Central to both lines' original plot was taking advantage of the valleys and low-lying breaks across mountain chains. Today's pathway reflects that choice with one prominent exception, Palisades Canyon west of Carlin. The Humboldt River created a narrow defile between butt ends of two mountain ranges, leaving just enough space for the original Central Pacific and eventually Western Pacific to creep through. A granite-ribbed chasm finds traffic rubbing shoulders through its watercourse. The off-cadence signature of square-nosed GEs out of North Platte mingles with the 3,600-hp beat of tunnel motors in Espee red and grey. Progress is reduced to a relatively mediocre 40 mph for the chasm's 10 to 12 miles.

In what appears an unlikely play in this parched frontier, a series of abbreviated girder bridges from the early 20th century directs rail across numerous bends along a rare desert stream that flows year-round through the canyon.

Going its independent way near Winnemucca, SP heads for Donner Pass, while the yellow diesels keep to a more westerly slant through Nevada Division's west end, among the most remote of UP's territories. Other than a dirt road or small-scale mining, there is literally nothing between Winnemucca and the high Sierra Nevada but uncluttered scenery and a guideline of steel ribbons.

Except for the modern motive power, the heavy steel and signal systems directed from afar, this sparsely populated region conveys a

100-year-old tintype. That is, until a colorfully bedecked stack train skoots across the distant horizon line lugging more tonnage behind more horsepower than even yesteryear's most visionary prophet could fantasize.

Because of physical trends across its western map, UP still favors the standard six-motored truck, high-horsepower unit of the past two decades, while other railroads now find B-B underpinnings more fashionable.

Southern Pacific maintains a small vested interest in UP property west of Winnemucca, using trackage rights to a lonely desert junction at Flanigan. There, home rails are joined for a connection with Oregon's traffic base. Local passing tracks at Jungo, Reynard or Sano—to mention but a few—are as likely to be occupied by cab stencils denoting assignment to Roseville or Eugene as they are yellow units serviced in North Platte.

Late afternoon finds a piggybacker racing across the emptiness of northern Nevada, its midnight departure out of Oakland just an expression of past tense. The track in the foreground is Espee in this area near Carlin, where SP–UP operate their single-tracked lines as one joint double-track railroad.

Just before the Golden State is reached, appropriately labeled Sand Pass offers some typical low-degree ascent and subsequent decline plus a 6,200-foot-long siding of the same name.

The limelight of jousting with the stoic Sierra Nevada generally falls to Southern Pacific's high-altitude run across Donner Pass, a locale not that far south of Union Pacific's crossing at Portola. That peak at Beckwourth Pass, where ex-WP rail passes through a tunnel, lies more than 2,000 feet below that of Donner. The differences in operating conditions are substantial, principally in snowfall. Whereas SP routinely uses round-the-clock plows and snowsheds to combat winter storms, UP is normally satisfied with a diesel's snowplow pilot—though it has problems of its own, generally related to rain.

With its purchase order, UP not only acquired a scenic wonderland but a harsh, demanding operating territory which can be as tough to maintain during the rainy season as it can be deceptively charming on a balmy afternoon.

On a fine summer's day, when mild canyon breezes gently twist pine trees under a cloud-bedecked sky and trains wander through the lengthy fissure in routine fashion, it's hard to believe that this part of Northern California has a schizophrenic mindset all its own. Not too many weeks ahead, heavily moisture-laden skies may turn this deep cleft in the mountains to a quagmire of falling rock and mud. Landslides all too easily triggered by crawling trains—Western Pacific archives have long recorded the events—throw nicely set schedules into hours of disarray. Then, slouching rain-coated figures in hi-rail vehicles or motor cars navigate ahead of each train, radios keyed open to broadcast the slightest hint of unstable hillside.

Blind hazards and soaked ground shaken by the tremors of passing trains are not always avoided. Over the years many a locomotive has collided with falling boulders, and many a freight car has taken the plunge into the Feather River's icy torrent. Changing a name from "Western" to "Union" doesn't automatically neutralize that particular issue. Money and capital improvements can only accomplish so much.

Curvature, not gradient, is the pacing limitation in Feather River Canyon despite the power of drawbar pull. And if everything goes right on a well-orchestrated day there will be no asterisks or notations appended to the train sheet. However, that doesn't always happen.

Outside of the Blue Mountains in Oregon, little mainline hauling on this vast railroad is so consistently restricted by nature. Practically all the canyon's 115-mile stretch is run at 30 mph or less, and there is a single section of just less than 70 miles between Poe Siding on the lower edge and Sloat Siding on the upper where 25 mph is a timetable's restrictive order.

What a contrast with the high plains where self-consciously important stack trains zip by telephone poles at high speed. Yet to get there from central California you have to pass through here. Without better connections and money the Wobbly wouldn't have been doing this either,

and even now its physical dimensions are being upgraded. Change, along with rail and new ties, is periodically required to keep the canyon competitive. UP these past two years has been pouring effort into the many tunnels that line the canyon's wandering trail. In between passing freights, the tunnel train, made up of a single unit and a complex looking set of rolling stock, scurries into nearby bores to expand its size for the bigger containers due tomorrow.

Motion to a railroad is more than just trains.

Until California invested in the giant dam near Oroville, WP rails took a right turn out of that town as they started up the canyon. Once the giant earthern coffer was constructed, a bypass became necessary. Now, yellow diesels, like their earlier counterparts, follow a more indirect course before plunging into the steep-walled mountain pass.

Unlike SP's Donner Pass which climbs along mountainsides, Feather River Division iron stays with the watercourse, though not necessarily at its banks. Along the lower reaches, at sidings like Pulga, Belden or Camp Rodgers, there is hardly a moment when some portion of an extended train

Curling through the upper reaches of the Feather River Canyon, an eastbound run gains momentum after having changed crews at nearby Portola. Within a half-dozen mileposts, the wooded zone will have given way to a flat, treeless valley to be followed in short order by the dry lakes of northwestern Nevada.

In ex-WP territory at Portola, California, a couple of freights exchange glances in a hurry-up panorama for modern train operations.

is not squealing or screeching around a sharply curved segment of welded rail. Especially those spindly-legged trailer flats or well cars.

Tangency? That's a word not commonly thought of around here. Passing one milepost, a worm-like set of cars may be almost touching the boulder-strewn watercourse; the next finds it peering down a 40-foot-high embankment from on high.

Despite its wandering habits, its penchant for quick, angular changes, Feather River Canyon track was built well enough to accept UP's 6900-class double motors. Western Pacific opted for four-axle motive power supposedly due to the hazards and restrictions imposed by canyon trackwork. So you can imagine the surprise when the long-framed D-Ds slipped into Stockton on a routine basis. Quite logically, today's burly SD60s and Dash Eights now find Feather River territory no different from anywhere else.

As tracks march toward a date with Nevada's expansive vistas, the barren, rock-ribbed outcroppings along the lower third of Feather River give way to evergreen-studded slopes. Eventually trains blast from a tunnel onto Keddie's well-known steel girder wye and California's Inside Gateway link.

Just as the term depression had become meaningful, a triumvirate of WP, Santa Fe and Great Northern had completed the Inside Gateway as a key to matching wits with Southern Pacific as a coastal competitor. Currently it has fallen upon hard times, providing little more than occasional interchange with Burlington Northern at Bieber, plus its own intermittent turn connecting with a Stockton-based local known colloquially as the *Valley Flyer.*

Soon, very soon, SD40 No. 3674 will be popping out of the short tunnel lying beneath its trucks as it rounds Williams Loop in Feather River country.

As of late 1988, a few dozen miles of CTC on the Bieber Subdivision north of Keddie became track warrant control, reflecting the Gateway's downgraded status. In today's marketplace, if it were all UP or all BN between Stockton and the Columbia River, the route might offer SP some serious competition between major Pacific Coast urban centers. But broken up as the Gateway is, and was, there are proprietary, conflicting aims which just don't mesh.

Not far east of Keddie lies Quincy Junction, a link to a local short line expectedly called the Quincy Railroad, a lumber mill's link with the outside world. Then it's on through the forested canyon to Williams Loop, California's other circular railroad artifact. Not many trains these days completely cross over themselves, but sometimes a unit grain train or a lengthy general freight accomplishes it. Ditto for a coal train out of Utah or a copper ore movement heading for Stockton.

UNION PACIFIC
UNION PACIFIC

Now widening somewhat, Feather River Canyon presents a series of intermittent meadows with narrow connectors including tunnels across its upper torso. Ultimately, Portola comes into view around a wide, gentle curve. Perhaps a westbound or two is chomping at the bit, waiting for an upbound movement to clear before setting off on an easier but just as slow descent of the canyon.

Unlike yesteryear when crews divided their time between Stockton–Oroville and Oroville–Portola, many of today's trains are handled on an interdivision pool basis all the way between the central valley terminal at Stockton and the upper canyon reaches at Portola.

Like many other terminals on this far-reaching rail empire, Portola is a few moments of lost momentum as men and women with overnight bags over their shoulders exchange places in the engine cabs of multi-unit lash-ups. Quite sporadically, a lineup makes mention of a caboose, but that would be on a low priority run, which would probably stick around Portola for a while, switching cars for the Reno Branch or storage tracks.

With every reason not to stay around—unless to let a soon arriving train clear—a quick highball befalls the majority of trains rumbling through Portola. Their destiny lies away from this lofty mountain pass.

A few more sharp curves east of Portola and then the easy flatness of the Sierra Valley provides what the canyon never could, more than a dozen miles of arrow-straight right-of-way, topped off by Chilcoot Tunnel through the apex of Beckwourth Pass. As the roadbed makes an abrupt turn northeast toward the Nevada state line, the 33-mile-long Reno Branch goes its independent way, a twisting thread through Sierra foothills. Weeknights this offshoot connects trailer flats and auto carriers with the main stem, from a small terminal just north of Reno's gambling emporiums.

Even after a decade of Union Pacific stewardship, it's hard to contemplate the Feather River Canyon as other than Western Pacific country, though memories of Perlman green road engines struggling for altitude grow hazier with time. Of the principal geographic features that made up that onetime independent railroad, such as Nevada's desert vastness, or the last leg into Stockton and Oakland, it was always the mountain sector that riveted attention among non-railroaders and operating people alike.

This is where echoes of history continue to bounce off sheer cliffs or play out among stands of evergreens. Yesteryear's GP35s and GP40s in their quadruple brotherhood sounded not unlike their same era brethren in six-axled SD40 form or the 16 turbocharged cylinders of today's SD60s. The flat-cadenced, rather subdued voice of Dash 8s is admittedly fresh in a dominant role when compared with the minority position that General Electric played on a WP locomotive list.

Much of that green-toned roster still serves on, now cast in armour yellow, scattered to the proverbial winds. Four-footed on a railroad that likes six, and aging by UP standards, ex-WP units can be found on branch

Opposite: Winter has descended upon the Feather River Canyon, and the famous bridge on a wye at Keddie, California, is surrounded by a blanket of white powder. Out of the thin sunlight of late afternoon, a hurrying freight speeds on its way to Portola where the next crew will come aboard to keep things moving.

Almost at an end . . . a half-dozen blocks from its Oakland terminal, UP runs down the middle of Oakland's produce/warehouse district, vying with automobiles for the right-of-way.

lines and hauling interchange through terminals though rarely seen on the railroad which they served tirelessly during the 1960s and '70s.

Anyone familiar with California's great central valley automatically understands UP characteristics between Oroville and Stockton. Flat, straight and fast portray an operational mode, except in cities, particularly Sacramento, where roadbed literally walks between houses and light commercial zones. The ex-passenger depot which once boarded ticket holders to the scenic pleasures of the *California Zephyr* now serves as a fashionable restaurant. Union Pacific frequently provides a show for its clientele.

Freed of Sacramento's restraining influence, trains race down the valley below, an area of good farmland with slowly encroaching urbanization.

Slowed again because of Stockton's street complex and an impending grade crossing with Santa Fe's main, trains crawl into the region's principal terminal, sandwiched between SP and the Chicago-based carrier.

Centered at Stockton is the Oakland Subdivision, which crosses coastal mountains to San Francisco Bay points. The onetime Tidewater Southern extends to Turlock from here, while some bits and pieces of the Sacramento Northern interurban lie northwest and east of the yard. Access to the latter is provided in some instances by running rights on both Santa Fe and Southern Pacific, significantly into Pittsburgh, the destination of the cross-nation, coiled-steel unit train from Pennsylvania. Entering Santa Fe territory at nearby Stockton Tower, these trains utilize 33 miles of running rights to the Port Chicago branch, a remnant of SN's juice system.

As the area's prime, and only, UP marshaling yard, the ongoing clatter of cars being classified floats over South Stockton on a continuous basis. Nearby, the Port of Stockton, an upriver port of modest dimensions, sometimes handles ore trains out of Utah, grain trains off the high plains, and coal in solid strings.

Eventually one last barrier stands between Stockton and the important traffic sources strung around San Francisco Bay: Altamont Pass. This final lap into Oakland's often fog-shrouded harbor can't compare with what Feather River Canyon demands, but it does create an abrupt change from the central valley's unrestricted tableland. Though just a few miles long, Altamont Pass is a challenge of sorts, a time of restrictive pace accompanied by shrieking flanges, as stack and van trains heel one way, then the other, on wandering steel.

It's always questionable to state with certitude the volume of traffic on a railroad, but a typical day's running would probably see a quartet of trains each way between Stockton and Oakland, the majority of it scripted. Eastbound there would be a trio of symbols departing Oakland between midnight and dawn; westbound arrivals cluster between the sun's rising and noon.

Beyond Altamont's grassy knolls a short open space exists through Livermore, and then an abbreviated canyon opens upon lower San Francisco Bay where the important San Jose Branch skips away at Niles Junction. Turning north, the main goes through wall-to-wall suburbia as only California can create.

The final play is atypical Union Pacific. Resembling a streetcar line more than main line, ex-WP rail splits a few city blocks east of tony Jack London Square. A few blocks further on, the waterfront looms, but first comes the wholesale produce mart, crowded with double-parked cars, scurrying forklifts and a few dozen vendors blocking the way, a general scene more reminiscent of New York's garment district than a West Coast port city.

Into this congestion rolls one of the railroad's finest, a trio of bluntly sculpted GEs leading a full-blown stack train. It will simply stop, blocked by boxes of produce and scampering forklifts. A portrait hard to imagine, as an impatient "Z" train, bell ringing, horn blasting, is totally immobilized on an asphalt strip that extends for less than the train's own length. Weekdays, usually in the morning, it's a routine event, quite a contrast with the Run 8 torrential pace west of Omaha.

Finally, reluctantly, the way is cleared. Brightly painted stacks of containers clatter across Espee's main line to the south and enter their own yard tracks, a slim grouping of curved rails flanked by shipside cranes, warehouses and the wind-blown waters of San Francisco Bay.

After that there is no more train, just a long collection of rolling stock waiting for the next short move. Perhaps to a ship, perhaps to another railroad or possibly to a piggyback terminal.

So ends a Pacific that was called Western and has become the Union.

There's still snow on the mountaintops as a solid set of SD40s brings an eastbound through the lower end of Portola, having just finished the long, slow climb up the Feather River Canyon.

Opposite: Dwarfed by the vast spatial feeling of the desert, a westbound drag scoots from siding to siding in a low-priority mode near Shafter, Nevada. In this day of hotshot freights, the train moves slowly due to its low status.

Four of UP's massive roster of SD40s speed east across a Nevada lakebed at Jungo Siding, a full trainload of imported automobiles trailing behind.

3592
3592
UNION PACIFIC

MOUNTAIN RAILROADING

AN APOCHRYPHAL STORY told around La Grande, Oregon, these days concerns the impact the local hill made on a visiting railroad official. Train crews have heard it repeated often, but if you're a stranger in town they don't mind dusting it off just once more.

It seems that soon after MoPac and Union Pacific tied the knot, an official from the midwestern road was riding an eastbound out of Hinkle in order to become more familiar with UP operations. Impressed by the slow, strikingly scenic climb up the Blue Mountain canyons, he was chatting unconcernedly as the lead unit popped over the grade's apex at Kamela and started down toward Nordeen Siding. As the first hint of this steep dropoff came into view, he reportedly leaped to his feet, uttered a few expletives and claimed that what lay ahead was more illusion than reality.

This is the way local railroaders like to impress outsiders about the workings of Oregon's vertical blockade, the Blue Mountains, which lie in the path of Union Pacific's route to the Pacific Northwest.

With few exceptions, UP has utilized modern locomotive design to overpower its need for helper engines. For instance, two of yesteryear's well-known helper districts, Sherman Hill and Utah's Weber Canyon, are now routinely conquered with head-end power only. But there are still some geographical barriers that force the UP to utilize helpers. Cajon Pass still echoes to the exertions of rear-end pushers on a routine basis, and then there's that 573-mile through helper assignment on extra-long stack trains between East Los Angeles and Milford, Utah. But the largest concentration of helper activity on today's Union Pacific is on the Nampa Division, which includes the railroad's crossing of the Blue Mountains. Currently, light, time-sensitive trains move across the mountainous portion of this division unaided, but the heavy tonnage trains still require helpers.

If contemporary diesel locomotive design can master the most famous of roadblocks, Sherman Hill, why can't it accomplish the same task in the Blues? Therein lies the tale of Union Pacific's busiest piece of single-track railroad outside of western Nebraska's coal train subdivision.

Opposite: A couple of trains pass on the outskirts of La Grande, Oregon, in August 1988.

For the past two days, a 100-car grain train has been making a steady, if unhurried, pilgrimage westward toward the Portland area. After hopping from siding to siding to dodge priority movements and, taking short rests at terminals like Green River and Pocatello, it is now pulling to a halt in Nampa, Idaho's slim yard. Halfway back, a brakeman cuts the trainline, freezing the rear half of the train in place after an explosive blast of air sets the brakes. Using a handheld radio, the trainman indicates to a trio of SD40s that they should pull ahead far enough to clear a mainline switch. Setting off with a fresh crew, the first half of the grain train is already rolling when a second set of units pulls through the mainline switch, ties on to the rear half of the train and begins pumping off the air brakes. Minutes later, it too will be highballing on west. Where once there was a single movement lighting a dispatcher's CTC board, now there are two, a measure taken out of respect for the Blue Mountains and a couple of troublesome cousins that lie ahead. A trio of helper districts is in the offing.

Until the last year or so, UP was boosting its very heavy trains, generally grain and soda ash types, across these mountains in 100-car increments, with four- and five-unit mid-train helper sets. Somewhat ponderous in performance, they often took 10–15 minutes just to clear a siding—irksome requirements on a district where perhaps 20–25 trains might answer the daily roll call. It is also no secret that mountain sections usually see trains bunched together, due to slower speeds and jumbled profiles.

Ever on the lookout for improved train performance, UP discovered that two short trains resulted in better handling, though two 3,000-hp helper units are still required 50 cars to the rear. Currently, it is standard procedure to split these hefty trains into two sections, take them across the entire 286-mile-long La Grande Subdivision, and rejoin them.

It is termed adaptability and few people have accused the modern-day Union Pacific of lacking this particular trait. When requirements change, when a better way is found, then new traditions will be formed. But simply reducing tonnage is not the only way to breach barriers. Make no mistake, the newest steel and concrete ties, as well as the latest in motive power technology, can be found in these mountains.

Computers and elegant programming notwithstanding, physical tensions on the Blue, like a dozen other western barricades, are stressful. A stroll through weeds by any mainline siding usually turns up discarded, broken coupler knuckles, a sure sign that something snapped as power was applied to a heavy train, made even weightier by the pull of gravity on the ascending two percent grade. No computer can accurately foresee this moment, nor can it experience the explosive blast of air pressure that follows, or understand the very human response as irritated curses resound across an engine cab.

With a half-dozen symbols, some hot, converging on the plugged spot from either end, computer electronics offer no solutions, only instant knowledge of the problem. Now only sweat and experience count, and

The easy part is over now. Having come up the Snake River from Nampa, Idaho, a westbound train has just about arrived in Huntington, Oregon, where it will pick up a two-unit helper for the next 20 miles or so.

only when air pressure once again registers the proper digits on a gauge, normalcy will have returned. Then the computer resumes its mastery as it adjusts and calculates to minimize the unexpected . . . which, if you comprehend railroading, is a norm.

Modern techniques of running a railroad are black box prone. Either that or you're an anachronism. Still they must be augmented by human factors, a reality that is nowhere so evident as on those mountaintops in northeastern Oregon.

Elsewhere on UP, long-forgotten surveys of another age skirted around impending barriers or found the path of least resistance. Contemporary packaged horsepower has been able to reduce yesterday's multiple helper districts to a handful, conquering them with 16-cylinder banks of energy and electrical current, but these facts are not the case in the Blues.

Traditionally, the diesel locomotives that UP has utilized in conquering obstacles like the Blue Mountains have been ones equipped with six axles. This preference for six-axled units has been continued in all of the company's recent locomotive purchases, in spite of the current trend among many railroads to order four-axled locomotives. An examination of UP's tonnage ratings table reveals the reasoning behind this tradition. The table displays how much a single unit can pull in a freight train averaging

On the La Grande Subdivision, a waiting freight (foreground) idles while one of three freights it will meet here scoots by in the background. Locale is Huntington, Oregon.

100 tons per car with output calculated at an 11-mph steady gait. A 3,500-hp, four-axled GP50 can lift 1,195 tons' worth of train between La Grande and the summit at Kamela, while an older six-axled SD40 or its Dash-2 variant, can tote 1,582 tons. A six-axled, 3,600-hp SD50 handles 1,814 tons and the even newer six-axled SD60, with 3,800 hp, can lift 2,056 tons per unit. A four-axled GP40 would be rated at 1,050 tons, a 3,000-hp, four-axled General Electric B30-7 rates drawbar effort of 1,241 tons, and so on. Mastery of mountain territory clearly is in favor of six-axled locomotive design.

Little wonder that Union Pacific favors this design. If they mixed six- and four-axled units in line they would need more units to conquer the mountain regions on the system. The six-axled unit is a hill climber, and with today's designs, a racehorse as well when opportunity arises. At track level, a set of six-axled units places more wear upon curves than a four-axled locomotive, while on tangent steel, the latter tends to hunt and wander slightly more. This leaves the railroad with few choices. While four-axled units may reduce the wear and tear upon sinuous mountain trackage, they are not as efficient as their six-axled brethren in terms of hauling tonnage.

Although that portion of the division west of La Grande is the most difficult to traverse, there are two other sectors where helpers are used, albeit generally on the rear end. In either direction between La Grande and Pendleton, trains of 4,800 tons or less do not require assistance, but on those exceeding this mark, helpers are a prerequisite. East of La Grande the criteria is 6,200 tons to Huntington, while on the reverse course it's again 4,800 tons from Huntington to La Grande.

On occasion a solo helper works on the Nampa Sub, shouldering behind westbounds through Glenns Ferry, Mountain Home and the few miles of undulating countryside. UP is very flexible in such assignments, even though helper service is concentrated in the Blue Mountains. Extra power is sometimes briefly seen elsewhere in times of special need. For instance, in early 1988 there were a few helpers working north of Las Vegas, generally around Moapa, hustling trains up Meadow Valley Wash!

The approach to helper country from Idaho's plains or, for that matter from the Columbia River side around Hinkle, is deceptively easy. Tidy, fast roadbed prevails across farmland and then in the wide canyons of the Snake River, gradually moving on through Nampa and beyond. Then near Huntington, Oregon, the railroad crosses the river and abruptly splits a

Drifting downgrade after having helped a grain train out of Huntington, a two-unit set of helpers returns for another train to aid.

Now this is what one expects to find in the mountains of western America! A trio of GE units serves as the centerpiece of a heavy train moving westbound between La Grande and Baker, Oregon.

brief crevice as the first hills are encountered. In the days of the steam engine, Huntington was a vibrant, pulsating terminal, active in all manner of comings and goings during an era when it took 10 or 12 hours to make a hundred-mile trip. Presently it contains a couple of tracks from the old yard, plays host to an occasional turn out of La Grande and is where helpers are tied to many westbounds. Otherwise it is just another long siding with power control switches.

From the 2,112-foot level of Huntington, the rails climb out through barren hills, occasionally hitting patches of 2.2 percent grade before cresting at Encina—3,968 feet—immediately followed by a descent into Baker on a 1.50 to 1 percent grade. Guided by their availability, some helpers on westbounds may be coupled in past Huntington, say at Weatherby or Nelson, possibly staying with the train all the way to La Grande. Eastbound, Quartz Siding, outside of Baker, is a favorite rendezvous, but as with all such placements, you never can be certain. A helper crew may be short on working time, or perhaps two or three grain trains might be clustered in one direction with power a bit tight, forcing a dispatcher to make the best choice, often eschewing routine.

Another grade lies between Baker and La Grande, peaking out at Telocaset Siding, which is approached from the west on a 1 percent grade, and from the east at 1.50 percent. That's why a helper out of Huntington may stay attached all the way to La Grande, a 100-mile journey through and over assorted ridges, descents and sharply defined clefts in a landscape of tumbled geography.

Then comes La Grande. Once its relatively modest length yard tracks were sufficient to contain trains of a past era. Fifty-foot boxcars, 81-foot trailer flats and their extended cousins have rendered these tracks obsolete. Because of this lack of space when trains stop to change crews, there is precious little room to stand around generating idle chitchat at the transition. Twin tracks extend four miles west and five miles east of the depot, creating some breathing room for those times when a group shows up. And that is quite often, for in accord with many a mountain railroad, trains have a way of bunching up between La Grande and Hinkle.

Blame it on the mountain.

Looking westward from La Grande at ground level, the roadbed apparently disappears borelike between two, almost vertical, pillars of Blue Mountain granite. On closer inspection, a nifty twist of tightly bent steel avoids tunneling and wiggles through a modest crack in the armor, immediately climbing toward the forested slopes ahead. At this point, already a half-percent upthrust is underfoot, and trains conform snakelike while hoggers search for a lower throttle notch as momentum bleeds off.

Ahead, around a sharp curve, two tracks forge into what the mountain will allow, one. Red over red glares forth in unequivocal terms, spawning a waiting game. Not far ahead is a solid string of auto racks rolling downgrade behind a trio of hefty Dash-8s in full dynamic brake mode. Twelve thousand horsepower singing in reverse, even that not enough to keep a few whiffs of brake shoe smoke from swirling in the mountain air.

Hundreds of miles away in Omaha, tiny round lights, products of long-distance links, depict this faraway scene in sanitized, flat expressions of control. No sound, no emotion, just dictation. Here we see the big picture—dozens of illuminated references stretching from the Mississippi to the Columbia Rivers. And while some of these symbolic references will bridge inches of wall space quickly, others in the cavernous, surreal room of electronic technology will linger much longer. Guess which ones are labeled Kansas or Nebraska Division, which one the Nampa?

Being held at Perry, just west of La Grande, is a fairly typical event for slower, normally heavy trains. The DS wants to give them a fair shot at keeping full throttle on the hill, and better to wait here than to experience every siding on the climb to Kamela. Crowding is a further consideration.

Two, perhaps three moves will glide by a stopped movement before a double signal displays red over green. A puff of exhausted fumes clears the stacks as thunder rises in a coordinated voice and wheels begin a plodding gait and soon a few thousand feet of train will have staked their claim to the Oregon Trail.

Lastly, a hard-driving duo numbered for the U30C class puts in an appearance, shoving hard into the final coupler, lending its muscle in a spirit of cooperation. Certainly it will be needed in this full engagement with a tough subdivision.

A hogger, temporarily over from the MoPac during the summer of 1989, was queried on how difficult it was to control tonnage on this Blue Mountain upthrust. The veteran runner, not quite willing to admit its challenge, replied initially that it was no more spirited than the hills of Missouri from whence he came. Later, in a bit of candor he admitted, "If I can run this railroad, I can run anywhere."

These western "hills" put on a tough show.

Fourteen ever-rising mileposts separate Perry from Kamela, as well as a 2.2 percent upgrade and a series of nearly perpetual curves. In wanting to determine what motive power is capable of, you test it here because Union Pacific's big units operate systemwide. Only a few roster occupants with four axles are expected to be routine visitors, although their capabilities are confirmed, just in case. And they do show up as uncommon travelers in this land of giants.

Performing well on the Blues is tantamount to general acceptance.

This is a cleverly crafted railroad dating from 1880–1883 when the Oregon Railway and Navigation Company set up local construction camps. Unlike some steel which was laid along ridges or blasted through tunnels, builders hereabouts took advantage of every nook and cranny, streambed, or soft opening in the Blue Mountain's armor to accomplish their goal. Frequently, choices were nil and although the line isn't reminiscent of a head-on assault, it owns many a deep, rock-lined cut or extended fill along its rather convoluted survey line. While Hinkle's retarder yard rests almost due northwest of La Grande, UP will be working its trains west, north, due east, south and then north again before ultimately setting on a final course toward Pendleton and the huge terminal beyond.

Never satisfied with its status quo, engine cab scuttlebutt has UP making long-range plans for tunneling the Blues, a lengthy bore several miles in length, that would lop off miles and time. Meanwhile, a 19th-century survey party set today's alignment.

Relatively modest in height, the Blue Mountains are characterized by their abruptness, unlike mountain chains further down the coast. La Grande is at 2,855 feet, and while Kamela tops out at 4,205 feet that altitude is covered mostly in the final 10 miles of struggle at a steady grade of 2.21 percent. The opposite flank, the Pendleton side, holds steady to that same climb for about 12 miles below the crest, reduces to 1 percent for another 20 miles, and then drifts generally downward to level off around the 1,000-foot marker.

"Mountain dispatcher . . . Omaha." A calm, disembodied voice floats out of a cab radio somewhere on the Blue Mountains. Omaha, there're no mountains around Omaha? Then realization hits; everywhere west is now a three-dimensional railroad reacting to two-dimensional visions.

On the westbound climb out of La Grande, those final three miles or so around Nordeen–Kamela are the ultimate test with dispatchers, who often keep in close touch via radio. Not so much for lightweights with their four-hp-per-ton strength, but for heavier trains. A six-degree curve, followed quickly by an eight-degree arc, test a prime mover's mettle as it heads on high, especially if you've been holed up on Motanic Siding, two miles below. Dragging out of this alley, perhaps on a wet day, or in a snowstorm, means that progress is best calculated at a crawl or on occasion, a stall. Assuming there's nothing hard on your heels you can back down a mile or so for a second attempt, something your fellow enginemen out there on the flat Nebraska Division never heard of. Only tensile strength of couplers and number of cars limit their exertions on the flats. Out here, gravity is a better known force.

Kamela is home to a long center-track siding, thrust amidst a seven-mile stretch of two-track running. Well polished, Kamela Siding is a favorite holding point for slower, longer trains. Long ones are hung out like an inverted vee, trainlines pointed down in both directions. Still, it only takes a fairly easy nudge to get moving again when a searchlight signal fixes you with its green okay.

In this slow, stop-wait-and-get-started-again theatre of train handling, many hoggers run their charges by ear rather than by meter. That was fine with the recently standard SD40s, but the newer engines pose a slightly altered state of affairs, especially on those big GEs. Engineers have learned to think differently because these engines, in going from Run 4 through Run 7, display no difference in tone, unlike the EMDs, whose engines are more noise-sensitive at varying speeds. The computers themselves come in for a bit of discussion, as an occasional delay in responding to controls can make an engineman edgy. Since a computer has a programmed mindset all its own, it functions on what it thinks is best, and then, not always as quickly as a human commands. For instance, upon leaving a siding on a steep downhill portion of the Blue Mountain grade, an engineer may initiate an early brake pipe reduction, but the computer holds off for a few seconds on its own. Meantime, tonnage continues pushing cars along a little faster leading to a slight feeling of apprehension until an electronic mind authorizes its own response.

The western slope of Blue Mountain territory is a real wanderer. Equally as steep for several miles as the opposite flank, it dives into an extremely narrow opening below Meachum, proceeds to make almost a complete walk around the compass and finally heads due north in the depths of Boston Canyon. All this wiggling is required to skirt a spur descriptively labeled Horseshoe Bend.

Ending—at least for the railroad—as quickly as it loomed large at La

3657

Grande, Blue Mountain country runs out at Gibbons where roadbed penetrates the upper Columbia River basin. Ahead, a vast expanse of not quite flat land spreads to a far horizon line, one now absent of vertical complexity. Much further away, down towards Pacific Coast waters, there are some awesome mountain barriers for other railroads to consider.

Union Pacific will manage to avoid all but the most modest hills as it races downriver to Portland and then Seattle, or through Spokane to the Canadian border.

This is its northwestern territory, the traffic of which is collated by nearby Hinkle's grasping retarders. Helpers, mountain break-in-twos and train-laced sidings become only memories rapidly fading from view behind the last trailing truck.

Now the obstacle course is over, physical trials giving way to a less demanding section of the Union Pacific. The lights back there in Omaha move a lot faster on this section.

"Mountain dispatcher, Omaha," has lost its luster to another wall panel further along in that schematic representing Western America.

One of the busiest stretches of single track on UP's system is the mountain territory between La Grande and Pendleton, Oregon. Trains sometimes sit for lengthy stretches while the mountain clears.

Opposite: After about two bends and a mile, this Nampa Division train has shed its flirtation with the Snake River and now heads inland toward La Grande and Hinkle's modern retarder yard.

9019 9019
9019
ROADWAY

NORTHWEST TERRITORY

UNION PACIFIC'S NORTHWEST dominion is a divided house, much of it relying upon easememt rights on another's property. On one hand there are 764 miles to Sea/Port Division, essentially a power-controlled type railroad linked with high speeds, a counterpart in status with those single-track lines west and south out of Salt Lake City. Hinged to port cities in Oregon and Washington, it provides what you might expect, TOFC/COFC traffic in abundance, solid cuts of auto racks behind powerful six-axled units, and the steady westward trek of unit-grain trains.

The other half, Spokane Division, with 1,138 miles under one management, generates a totally different vision, one somewhat unusual for the railroad. Centralized Traffic Control is a minor player in this region; even automatic block signals are in short supply. Branchline running abounds and Track Warrant Control (TWC) is the symbol most often seen in the division's operating timetable. Its format, then, is mostly tap roots, contributing to the traffic flow in multiple ways, but without the racetrack look you come to associate with most of Union Pacific.

In terms of a crude framework, think of the line coming across Idaho and the Blue Mountains as a shaft with its upper end extending northwest into the major classification yard at Hinkle. Union Pacific's northwest territory then forms a sort of shallow "Y" hinged from this anchor. Sea/Port Division creates the left branch, Spokane Division its right. One flows downriver to Portland and from there to the Seattle–Tacoma region, while the other reaches north through eastern Washington into Idaho's upper panhandle and touches the Canadian border.

Hinkle's sprawling eastern Oregon terminal, like North Platte's, is lodged far away from population centers. Like much of Union Pacific today it is a contemporary investment completed in the late 1970s. Operationally, considering how area lines expand west and northwest, it couldn't be more properly positioned. If someone with a knowledge of railroading were shown a system map and asked to choose a setting for an

Opposite: Once the steel trail gets over Oregon's Blue Mountains, the downriver path to Portland is easy going along the Columbia River. Here, a westbound run speeds in the vicinity of The Dalles.

The last car's been sent over the hump and a twin set of engines is about to be sent out to gather in another train for switching at Hinkle, Oregon.

important northwest classification center they would probably let their finger rest on Hinkle.

Bailey Yard was hardly off and running when dirt began flying on the upper Columbia Plateau, bulldozers and huge earth movers creating the kind of retarder yard that would key northwest movements. It was a visionary step toward the northern tier's future with no regrets incurred.

Sharply contrasting with steel that follows the Columbia River along the onetime Oregon River Railroad and Navigation Company route, the Spokane Division behaves like a page out of 1960s' railroading. The backbone is a subdivision of the same title which bends away slightly northeast from Hinkle, protruding some 327 miles to the Canadian border in a somewhat understated manner. Fifteen miles of Burlington Northern, running rights are needed to close a gap between the subdivision's two principal sections south of Spokane. Without BN's roadbed UP could accomplish the feat on its own more circuitous route as it approached metropolitan Spokane.

Like trackwork north and south of Pocatello the eastern part of Washington State is four-axle land. Not completely, for older six-motored types, SD40s and U30s, are normal on through freights, but the plentiful secondary lines host a lot of power numbered below 2200. GP35s, GP40s, and

Hinkle services several hundred units each month including this U30C on a July evening in 1988.

others of intermediate physique keep the rails polished north of Hinkle.

Branchwork east of Spokane Division's backbone taps the rounded hills of Palouse country, an area not overly blessed with rainfall, though ideal for raising wheat and other related crops. Perhaps it should be called Kansas with hills. Forests check in as the Palouse River spills into Idaho. The dust of scurrying combines shifts to the sights and smells of the woodcutter as timber mills replace grain silos on a waybill.

The urgency which attends train movements between large cities is not that apparent on the Spokane Division, which functions as feeder, not super mover. Intermodal loadings, which dominate traffic on primary routes, are virtually unknown in eastern Washington.

Conforming to the railroad's image, engineers become adept at train-length switching moves. The omnipresent radio has made hand signals virtually archaic, but not the skill of mastering five figures of horsepower and a hundred or more car lengths of slack. As runthroughs complete their chores at junctions and connections, the turns put in an appearance, led by intermediate-rated diesels.

Extended black tank cars are picked up by locals, along with empty hoppers from the spine. Many a tiny Palouse community boasts a spur with pumping gear where agricultural chemicals and petroleum products are transferred on the way in, and where grain silos at the opposite end generate an annual harvest. During summer's long daytime, train lists handled by any one of the area's supporting cast can vary considerably.

Bedded overnight in Moscow, Idaho, one of these locals is on its way to Colfax before local restaurants have finished serving breakfast. Waiting there is the daily script. Some days it reads more like a switch list, but then a local is supposed to be like that. Yesterday, 104 empties, chiefly covered hoppers, were theirs at Hooper Junction, dropped off by a through freight.

Its rail too light for six-axled power, the Spokane Division's Tekoa Branch is host to GP38-2s, as the daily local switches cars from a grain elevator.

Late summer is at hand and after weeks of hauling fertilizer and other supplies the tide is turning to outbound loads. The twin GP38s working this turn had their hands full with that extended group of empties as they came through the hill country of the Palouse.

Lest an erroneous impression of Spokane Division's personality be created, consider how this local's crew receives its instructions. A junction where the Tekoa and Moscow branches blend, Colfax long ago ceased to mount train order signals. Call it a VDT or a CRT, a TV set and its connected printer provide all instructions necessary to run today's train, linked as they are to UP's central command post. The human factor may be aboard trains, but elsewhere computer-generated monitoring is a norm. This isn't 1960s' railroading. No way.

Today turns out to be a bit modest; a dozen cars come out of Colfax; switching occurs at a half-dozen places, and about 20 cars arrive at the mainline junction—an easy task for a dual lashup of two GP38s. Yesterday, though, that was a different matter. With over a hundred cars to haul through the twisting countryside, 4,000 hp was just barely enough.

Palouse country branches are pretty much like that, tied to agriculture's seasonal peaks and valleys of carloading. Off west, the Yakima Branch has similar traffic flow with an industrial mix thrown in, though it lacks the pastoral beauty. The Palouse is early 20th-century grain silos, wandering track through hillsides alive with waving stands of wheat, timber trestles and slow trains, a creation of a Union Pacific rarely depicted on the famous annual calendar.

Given relatively modest limits on motion—40 mph from Spokane to Canada's border, 50 mph south to Hinkle—the attributes of a Dash-8 or an SD60 would be underutilized on the Spokane Division. Power is dominated by older 3,000-hp types, the ubiquitous SD40 and its equally able but different looking cousins, GE's U30C and C30-7. They're well suited for this service, a bit shopworn with age but more than adequate at a drawbar. And while container cars, trailer flats and every other style of contemporary car design gets into Spokane, they don't come in solid cuts. Elsewhere they may be looked upon as the pampered darlings of trunkline railroading, but in the far north they're mingling with lumber, grain, boxcars and general merchandise. It all changes somehow at Hinkle.

The daily local working between Sandpoint and Eastport, Idaho, rolls across a bridge at Bonner Ferry after spending almost an hour switching a big lumber mill.

On a rainy August day in the Northwest, a couple of GP40s and a GP38 work the Camas Prairie Railroad out of Lewiston, Idaho.

Two paired acronyms, HKCP and CPHK, are the principal players between Hinkle and the north end where Canadian Pacific interchange takes place. Tasked to a roughly 14-hour schedule in either direction, these through moves will be supplemented by a Spokane–Hinkle run each way plus whatever extras are needed during seasonal peaks.

A lot of carloadings flow forth from the Palouse and from forests northeast of Spokane. The road to Canada covers the old Spokane International, a short line taken over during the 1950s. Once part of downtown Spokane, today's SI Yard is a new one on the eastern outskirts, a namesake remnant of a line that UP desired as an entree to Canadian business.

North of Spokane, wood products replace agriculture as a primary source of loadings. Complementing the two daily runthroughs are several turns. One turn serves the Coeur d'Alene branch, while another duo originates out of Sandpoint further up the line. There's a turn serving mainly timber mills between there and the border while a second provides similar duty along the opposite path.

Shortline St. Marie's River Railroad connects with the Wallace Branch, where once every other day turnaround service was operated to lead and silver mines in that picturesque Idaho town. Currently, Wallace is a once-a-week trip. The daily branch local usually stops far short of that destination before coming back to high iron at Manito.

Closer to Hinkle's sorting bin is a branch that reaches into the foothills around Walla Walla, Washington, and the Riparia branch which connects the Camas Prairie's UP–Burlington Northern partnership at Lewiston. A daily train brings out a fairly hefty amount of tonnage from this source, normally after midnight.

Individually, there is no great torrent of activity from any of the Spokane Division branches. Collectively, they provide a steady source of action for the crest at Hinkle's retarder yard bowl.

In contrast, the Sea/Port Division is a typical extension of Union Pacific's present-day likeness, a saga of self-important stack trains, fast-flowing pig trains and a place where even the casual freight makes time, all to a six-axled tune of relentless progress. Curiously, the division owes as much to the directions of Burlington Northern dispatchers as it does to its own. On the trunk route, Portland–Seattle, 144 mileposts out of 181 are listed as being run under a BN rulebook, while on the Oregon Trunk, that twisted, canyon-plagued track into central Oregon, the Bend Branch, is 151.9 miles long, listed in its totality as "via BN." Trains en route that way are required to get their clearance from the BN at nearby Dalles.

The Grays Harbor Branch in western Washington explains that of its 58 miles all but five are maintained by BN.

Mention the "water level route," and longtime railroad enthusiasts might think of New York Central's ride along the Hudson River. Up here in the Northwest there are two railroads, both hugging the Columbia River's widely spaced banks that are equally affiliated with that term. Union Pacific occupies the Oregon shore; Burlington Northern is found on the Washington side.

From the perspective of Hinkle's dry grass plain, the possibility of a great river but 18 miles and a dozen signal lights off west seems unlikely. Nevertheless, in that short span, the 184-mile Portland Subdivision swings alongside the Columbia paralleling every crook and bend in the Northwest's famous channel to Portland, where steel forges inland to Albina Yard.

Hinkle, at 635 feet elevation, and Portland, at 200 feet, are separated by just under 200 miles. Given its immense dimensions and geological age, the Columbia River accomplishes its turns and twists across wide, shallow arcs which a railroad can mimic as long as it stays in the trough. Like Nebraska and Kansas mainline territory, this is runnin' country, not the arrow-aligned tangency that lets rolling wheels notch 70 and hold, but it's fast, creating just enough awareness to make a hogger use a brief 5- or 10-pound reduction on a fairly routine basis.

Between Hinkle and The Dalles two branches and BN's Oregon Trunk slip away south, discovering niches to escape by. While the yellow units take Deschutes River Canyon's arduous trip to Bend in regular stride, the other two operate by "General Order," a phrase meaning service is irregular or as necessary. The lines are typically more active in summer months when local crops are harvested, although lumber activity keeps the Heppner Branch working at other times. A local or so out of The Dalles complements what is essentially a mainline panorama.

Three major port cities and a specialized grain facility are the reasons Sea/Port Division is a vital element in Union Pacific's strategic thinking. High-priority schedules with containers, trailers or solid blocks of auto racks leave or converge on Portland, Tacoma and Seattle with daily regularity. Upriver from Portland the specialty of Kalama is grain off-loading, the goal of 100 percent covered-hopper trains made up from Midwest grain silos. Most hotshots bypass Hinkle, taking on fuel and exchanging crews while holding mainline steel. From there they either head "downriver" or tackle the "mountain." Mingling with this high-profile calling are general freights and loadings off the Spokane Division, the ones destined for cutting up on the hump.

Daily traffic is about equally split between Portland–Seattle and Portland–Hinkle in frequency, roughly a dozen through the Columbia gorge, par to the north.

Down by the waterfront—in this instance the Willamette River—lies Portland's highlight, Albina Yard. Like all major terminals, its focus has gradually shifted toward TOFC/COFC action, with the boxcar trade taking a backseat. A few minutes of terminal delay at Albina is more likely to be tolerated on a seven-day-a-week Portland–Hinkle (PDHK) freight than it would on a nightly PDSEZ (Portland–Seattle) schedule with its urgent cargo of highway trailers. The area, including Portland's docks and the port of Kalama further down the Columbia River, is a major player in the grain trade. A large fraction of Albina's yard tracks are usually full of covered hoppers working this commerce.

Frequently, westbound trains bypass Albina for a satellite facility, Kenton Yard in North Portland. The area's rail map traces out a thin triangle tied together by Albina, Kenton and Troutdale to the east. Kenton's main function is sorting out grain, soda ash and bulk traffic; it's also a base for the industrial district around it. While the majority of area trains originate in Albina, some bypass it through the northern yard. Lighter tonnage moves generally slip out of Albina to the south then turn east toward Troutdale, a line which includes a one percent incline in that direction. To avoid this climb, heavy tonnage trains receive clearance to go by way of Kenton and the north routing as they head toward Hinkle.

For a brief stint the Albina-Troutdale path parallels Portland's recently constructed light rail line, which crowds a freeway in a wide cut directed toward the city's downtown, a true transportation corridor.

Avoiding transfer costs, Pier 6 northwest of Albina provides a direct connection between ship and container car, a method currently gaining wider acceptance as ocean-railborne volume increases. In late 1989 Albina's container facility was functioning at 150 percent of its rated capacity.

Like most major terminals connected to big cities, there is a rhythm associated with Albina's timecard. The second trick routinely processes 8–12 trains during its high-tension shift, often as much as the first and third shifts combined, demonstrating how closely today's railroad must master the challenge of time. This very same surge is found at all intermediate points—Green River, Salt Lake City, Pocatello and everywhere west.

Hardly atypical is that concentration of moves at Albina.

The run north to Tacoma–Seattle is done on someone else's railroad, the Burlington Northern. Union Pacific shares space and train orders from the Columbia River to Tacoma where it climbs back upon its own roadbed. A double-track layout, this is one of those places where you just wind up and go, especially for UP. There is one exception, Kalama's big grain terminal not far from the Portland area, which is the object of many a solid

North Platte–Seattle hotshot, the NPSEX rolls out of Portland's Albina Yard with a load of Seattle-bound traffic. The route is mostly over BN roadbed.

Business is good on Union Pacific's waterfront locations, especially for containers. The smell of salt air mingles with diesel exhaust here in Seattle where, after a quick inspection, three big units will be on their way east with a stack train.

grain train out of the Midwest. Many of those covered hoppers at Albina or Kenton have been or will be hauled downriver to ships waiting along the Columbia's wide banks.

Both Tacoma and Seattle provide voluminous car numbers to the car monitoring center in St. Louis, evidenced by as many daily trains between the area and Portland as there are connections up the Columbia between Portland and Hinkle. Tacoma's past was as a bulk-type port; today its legacy revolves around container traffic, somewhat ironically, for a major off-loading dock now exists on former Milwaukee Road (a railroad that couldn't make it) yard tracks. Full-length trains now roll onto BN and UP iron courtesy of a former carrier that starved for lack of carloadings!

Like every other major harbor on the Pacific Coast, Seattle projects a jumbled mass of industry and international trade paraphernalia: cranes, floodlighted nights, huge rectangular boxes stacked in threes and fours, literally an anthill of transport forms.

Almost on that crowded waterfront is Argo Yard, positioned not only for cargo working the piers but for the burgeoning Seattle economy as well. Like so many other once individual cities, Seattle–Tacoma is now expressed in a single statement as suburbs become one extended mural.

A small engine terminal at Argo turns units, checks their vitals and sends them back to wherever they originated. But if anything more is necessary it will probably be way back upriver to Hinkle.

The railroad's Condensed Service Plan, a printout of regularly sched-

uled trains, indicates a solid maritime connection running just about every day from Seattle or Tacoma—sometimes from both—along with the standard piggybacks such as the SECSZ (Seattle–Canal Street). In many ways, Union Pacific in Seattle is Union Pacific anywhere, a striking example of staying competitive in a constantly evolving world.

Think now of a moonstruck night upriver on the Columbia. Sparkling flecks of light bounce off wide-flowing water as 12,000 hp choreographed in unison speeds toward Portland. Perhaps heavy fog is blanketing Seattle, turning Argo Yard quiet in its sound-absorbing grip. A Sandpoint-based turn is unhurriedly switching a lumber mill at Bonners Ferry, while just a few yards away Burlington Northern flies by with a 90-car rig, swathed coupler to coupler in pig flats.

A half-dozen four-axled jobs are out probing the Palouse countryside, nothing individually great but the makings of a train as they collect in Hinkle's bowl. There on the flat grassland of eastern Oregon a hotshot has just drifted to a fuel rack, its trainline emitting a slight sigh of air as it pauses for 10 minutes before dashing off again.

Take away the scenery and this could be UP anywhere. Include the unique background, and it's the Northwest Territory.

Twilight settles over the lower Columbia River near Hood River, Oregon, as a westbound mixed freight heads toward Portland with a slow freight.

9315
9315
UNION
PACIFIC

IDAHO AND BRANCH LINES

MIDMORNING FINDS Emmett, Idaho, embroiled in its small town tempo. A few people wait in line for a bank teller, a hardware store manager dusts shelves, perhaps a car salesman rushes out to hail someone pausing before his well-waxed models. Meanwhile, a block from Main Street, a pair of two-unit sets of UP's four-axled roster members is being primed to head overnight turns, one for the Idaho Northern Branch, one for New Meadows.

This is a different Union Pacific from that publicized on its annual calendars, not exactly backwoods but a bit rustic by comparison. For example, each of these branch runners will pull a high-cupola caboose, as five minutes shaved off an exchange of crews by end-of-train devices has no meaning here.

In Idaho, there are several "Emmetts," modest-sized communities providing a base for UP locals. These are still important sources in an octopus-like gathering network that once blanketed the state. As steel has been withdrawn to mostly trunkline status throughout UP's system, Idaho has been an exception, still maintaining a fair number of connecting links which plug into terminals at Nampa, Pocatello, and Idaho Falls.

Most of Idaho's secondary lines see service "as needed." The state has a high percentage of agricultural activity, thus the peaks and valleys of demand that go with it. Most weeks may see possibly one, perhaps two, trains wending their slow ways from town to town, bringing along empties, toting a few loads away—barely enough action to keep rust from forming. Then there's the "season" when one of those outlying track segments may contribute the equivalent of two or three siding length movements in a few days, generally in mechanical reefers. That solid consist of orange-yellow reefers slipping east off Sherman Hill and into Cheyenne was most likely built in Idaho, perhaps further back in Washington.

While southern Idaho mostly produces farm crops for UP, timber provides the railroad with a livelihood on some of its other branches, such as the Idaho Northern branch. Heavily forested slopes lie north of Boise and on up through panhandle country to the Canadian border, serving as

Opposite: About a half hour earlier, an eastbound "Z" train had cleared Pocatello yard so this PCNP (Pocatello–North Platte) train could start its run. Topaz siding, Idaho.

a base for wood flats and bulkhead cars in trainload proportions, their stacked packages of cut lumber wrapped in self-promoting logos of plastic. On a more localized path, there is a nice volume of business for wood chip cars, high-sided, open-topped bins that shuttle between mills hauling the specialized products each produces.

Identified by a heavy preponderance of such rolling stock, accompanied by a pleasant, faint odor of cut wood, entire trains are spawned from northwestern junctions and yards, fed in part by the branches. It's never difficult to identify their origins, even when bunched together on the plains of Nebraska.

Putting aside such musings, let's return to Emmett, where GP40 No. 655 and GP38-2 No. 2042 are prepared to lead the every-other-day turn on its jaunt up the Idaho Northern's (IN) scenic trail to Cascade. The first unit is ex-Western Pacific property, long since moved away from regular mainline assignments.

Once extending several miles beyond its present terminus to McCall, the IN once rather routinely created 85-car-length trains of logs, cut lumber, and even cattle. Today's version will on occasion haul logs but primarily brings empties inbound, cut wood and chip cars outbound. Tonnage often runs between 2,500–4,000 tons on the downhill return trip, more than enough to warrant the use of retainers on an 18-mile stretch of descending grade along the Payette River Canyon.

Emmett is located in a flat zone of farmland whereas the land northward turns mountainous. After jostling a couple dozen empties equally distributed between flats and wood chip cars, the local eases out of town, several street crossings' worth of air horn play announcing its departure. Farms soon give way to foothill orchards, then to the beginnings of a sharply framed river course, which the rails will accompany for several dozen of the most scenic miles the Union Pacific encounters. Trainmen are said to bid this job purely for its outstanding setting. In winter they might have second thoughts, as snow is said to "get belly deep."

For a while, the train rolls along Black Canyon Reservoir at a nice, casual gait. The world of branch lines is unhurried with reliability far more important than speed, which in any event would be impossible. The turn now is pretty much off on its own, freed from the concerns about competing use or opposing movements. There is a radio, of course, but there are no cab signals or roadside block signals, only the general order instructions which provide the turn with uncontested control of the branch until it returns to Emmett tomorrow.

A transition from farmland to foothill grasses and on into timberland is pretty much complete by Horseshoe Bend, 22 miles from Emmett. Now, track will twist and turn with every abrupt change in the fast-flowing Payette River, whose narrow watercourse leaves just about enough room for the railroad and a state highway. A small Boise-Cascade Company mill at Horseshoe Bend is switched on the way up, some full chip cars being pulled away from a loader, empties positioned in their stead. On the return trip tomorrow, these loads will be picked up, completing a cycle of switching services that is a necessary part of the mill's production needs.

Incomparable is perhaps the best adjective to use in describing the line as it plunges headlong into a river canyon beyond Horseshoe Bend. There are few places on the Union Pacific that exceed the Idaho Northern branch in sheer unadorned elegance, as it caters to every whim of a pastoral stream. A steep-sided "V" brings about a hard-won climb with no room to maneuver in the river canyon beyond Horseshoe Bend. In consequence, there is a 20-mile section of really steep assault, almost half of which hovers near three percent.

There is no constant tattoo of diesels off canyon walls, more like intermittent bursts, for a combination of radical curvature and arcing climb prescribe a deft throttle hand, shifting among notches several times between each milepost number.

A standard timecard is OS Emmett at 11 A.M., arrival in Cascade at 3:30 P.M. Given that Horseshoe Bend is normally the only interim stop, such predictability is almost certain.

One of the most picturesque of UP's Idaho branch lines is the Idaho Northern Branch, which sees a train up one day, and one down the next. Within a mile of this site, this loaded train will stop and turn up retainers, since the two units do not have enough dynamic brake capacity to hold the train's speed in check on the steep downgrade.

Lying astride a high meadow, surrounded on all sides by heavily forested mountains, Cascade is a terminus with a fair-sized Boise-Cascade mill as its principal employer. The whining buzz of saw blades is constant as the tandem of Nos. 655 and 2042 draws alongside. Already the caboose has been dropped off a few hundred feet back to allow switching room.

For the next hour or so, an orderly, persistent ballet of channeled movement will occur. Shove these cars down a track, pull others out, then reshove the original ones back, and so on. With switch list in hand, a conductor and his two brakemen make sense of it, placing each car in line where it's supposed to be, empty or loaded. Then off to a nearby motel until early tomorrow morning where, underneath cloudy skies, a second ritual dance will be performed, this one putting together a train. During the night, more cars will have been loaded, requiring additional chores at the mill before moving out.

A half mile or so past the mill the branch officially ends, marked by a side track holding a couple dozen empty log racks in UP markings, a somewhat unusual breed of rolling stock for a major railroad these days. They don't appear to be in bad shape, and inquiry elicits a response that they receive occasional use on the branch, an unexpected sort of traffic on a railroad that ordinarily rolls two-dozen stack trains and 12,000-ton coal titans around on a 24-hour watch.

By the time it's ready to roll, the Idaho Northern turn has nine loaded wood chip cars along with 15 flats of green wood positioned between engine and caboose. It's explained that "green wood" is being forwarded elsewhere for drying, a capability not available in Cascade. Rather surprisingly, average weight per car is around 90 tons; flats weigh between 70–80 tons, and chip cars roughly 100 tons. That's almost as heavy as a coal car!

Despite an almost total downhill return to Emmett, tonnage is a rather significant concern, principally in terms of braking ability. While UP's timetable instructions mention retainer use on at least three mainline sectors, the Idaho Northern is but one of two branch lines where such ideas are advanced. The other branch is an iron ore source in southern Utah.

The use of retainers is necessitated by an 18.8-mile segment of steeply sloping line along the river between Smiths Ferry and Banks, half of which descends three feet every 100 feet. Rules call for all retainers to be set in the HP position, dynamic braking or not, unless there is five or more horsepower-effective dynamic brake per trailing ton. With today's 24 cars plus caboose totaling around 2,400 tons, that requirement could only be met with enough units to exceed 12,000 hp. A 2,000-hp GP38 plus a 3,000-hp GP40 fall far short of that standard, so retainers must be set at Smiths Ferry. Even then, if any brake pipe reduction exceeds 15 pounds, there is a mandatory halt for inspection along with brake system recharging prior to proceeding.

Rolling downhill at a pace slower than the previous day's ascent, the Idaho Northern train will tie up at Emmett by late afternoon, its crew

Log racks don't get much use on the UP these days, except on the BN–UP jointly owned Camas Prairie. Nevertheless, an occasional demand for them finds the UP ready and willing, as here in Cascade, Idaho.

The northern Idaho branchline's existence spins around wood products including a lot of wood chip cars. Basically a regional move, the chip cars move between lumber mills and processing plants in the Northwest. Cascade, Idaho, 1989.

members quickly off duty and homeward bound. Later, a turn will be over from Payette's mainline connection, bringing in the next day's flats and chip cars, taking away today's loads, as well as switching a local mill and industries.

The northwestern branch line of today is typically a specialist, its continued existence dependent upon a particular industry, or perhaps even a single firm.

Another wood-bearing branch line, the trail from Emmett to Rubicon, actually parallels the Idaho Northern, lying a few rugged hilltops away to the west. Further north, the Joseph Branch extends from La Grande, Oregon, and has its own program of lumber mills and associated consists.

Characteristically, trains on these feeder lines run six days a week, either Monday–Saturday or Sunday–Friday. They climb the canyons and mountainsides one day with empties and return the next with loads, primarily anything that can be related to wood products. While most cut or formed timber moves throughout the nation, chips are a regional business, shuffled along for relatively short distances across Oregon, Idaho, and Washington.

Away off east, and considerably south, another spate of UP lines plays its version of the IN. Here, raising food is the significant contribution.

It is late August in Rupert, Idaho. Languid night air hovers over a town fast winding down toward midnight. Splitting the small city in two, UP's Twin Falls Branch will be contributing a trainload or two to the flow of mainline traffic in the next 24 hours. Little more than a dozen miles off the Nampa Subdivision, Rupert is a breeding ground for more than a single movement this time of year. Mechanical reefers, their steady hum splitting the nightly solitude, fill spurs throughout a long, flat valley that extends toward Twin Falls, with 74 miles of track warrant control holding sway. Here also is the North Side Branch, equally as long, where operation is by General Order, the two creating stub ends through richly productive farm fields. Also impacting side tracks are long strings of covered hoppers in for other products.

An hour before tomorrow's date arrives, seven diesel units are sitting at Rupert, three idling, the others silent, all being logged in Omaha's ever-attentive computer memory. This is a land of second-class freights, obvious by a quartet of cabooses shoved into a nearby stub. An ancient wooden depot remains, totally dark and obviously abandoned, replaced by a much smaller metal structure opposite.

Momentarily, a few shadowy figures emerge from the new structure, cross a couple of tracks, then mount a set of two idling engines, one a flat-faced 2400 series from Erie, the other a more familiar SD40 from La Grange. No new power lying around here. Ten- to 15-year-old, essentially healthy locomotives are a much better fit for assignments that center upon secondary terminals like Rupert. There are no 15,000-mile monthly shifts to be rolled off around these parts.

Quickly grabbing a caboose, the local soon begins its nocturnal trip

Waiting for a trip up a branch line, a two-unit set of four-axled power waits at Emmet, Idaho.

west. Poking into packing sheds, shifting cars at a shipper's request, gradually building to 50-plus car lengths as it moves on, the local will stay busy right through dawn's first light. As the sky shifts from watery grey through brilliant red to blue, the ritual plays on. Each small town receives attention in its turn, a slow, steady progression that skips to the next, then the next after that.

By late morning, the branch worker has returned home, working a bit harder with a decent sized set of cars in tow as it greets the yard limit sign at Rupert.

Already a message has gone out: Extra 3325, Rupert to Pocatello, is called for 1 P.M. The journey continues, though now more class-conscious, for 13 miles ahead at Minidoka a switch to the main line beckons the Extra toward Pocatello's ever-hungry retarders.

Idaho Falls, some 50 miles north of Pocatello, is the center for another clutch of branchline moves. Passing through Idaho Falls' modest sized yard, actually a couple of long tracks, is a low-density main line north to Silver Bow, Montana, while a half-dozen branches penetrate the area to either flank. Home for a modest cadre of diesels, its servicing tracks display a sand tower and tank-car-style fueling facility. While the through moves have six-axled power, the local runs get four-axled sets, standard on most UP support routes in Idaho and Washington.

Six-motored units would be equally at ease on just about all local roadbed, but smaller motive power offers a more economical accounting and, in some instances, easier rail wear. Nor should we ignore the dictate of UP's locomotive management system, "Don't underpower, don't overpower."

In places like Idaho Falls, where a proliferation of branch activity is blended with main iron, a mixture of breeds is the rule; usually, Geep 38s and 40s for the branches, while SD40s and U-boats combine in lashups of three and four on mainline runs between Pocatello and Montana.

A pattern that emerges throughout UP's system finds turns toiling from either terminal of lengthy subdivisions or penetrating into branches, while through trains take up the slack at in-between spots rather than have a single extra work end to end. The Montana Subdivision through Idaho Falls pretty well illustrates that concept. It stretches across 255 miles, bonding Pocatello's hump yard to Silver Bow, just outside Butte. A daily heavy freight works in either direction on a through basis, supplemented most days by an ore train, loads north, empties south. Illustrating a regional thrust to traffic, the ore originates at Soda Springs on the Pocatello Subdivision, creating one of those heavy tonnage affairs that shuttles between its source and a copper concentrator near Butte.

North of Idaho Falls, a local proceeds up the main line to Hamer and then back. From the north end, a similar type is called out of Silver Bow; it works south as far as Dillon before skipping home with whatever it gathered. That leaves a roughly 100-mile gap for the through trains to service—but in a zone where running, not work, is dominant.

Although the Montana Subdivision is listed as a main line, it is not a high-density type. Trains move along very nicely with mostly track warrant instructions north of Idaho Falls. Typical of secondary routes, track speed is set at a maximum 40 mph.

Another daily local leaves Idaho Falls at midday, working northeast to Ashton before heading back to home base. "As needed," a phrase denoting an irregular scheme of dispatching, is conferred upon several other lines which radiate from Idaho Falls' central position. A minor network exists; some lines are merely elongated stubs whose entire length will be run under "yard limits"; others are of modest dimension, such as the Aberdeen Branch which covers 35 miles of farm field destinations. Then there's the 52-mile extension to Arco, the West Belt of 11 miles, and the East Belt of 38 miles. Typically, there is no regular pattern of service on these lines, though sometimes in late fall when sugar beets and potatoes are being harvested, there may be daily extras.

Normally the Silver Bow–Pocatello trains are able to handle traffic brought into Idaho Falls for forwarding, but in late fall a full-blown daily freight may originate in town and go to Pocatello's hump yard as agricultural business rises to a seasonal peak.

The autumn sugar beet harvest brings to life sidings and stubs that have lain dormant much of the year. Suddenly springing into action, they become crowded with three- and four-bay hoppers looking for business. Solid trainloads of heavy, bulky beets trundle to local sugar mills which see action only a few weeks each year. Filling sidings, the somewhat sluggish movements are kept separate from the high-profile, city-to-city types.

Union Pacific's mainline thrust from high plains country through Idaho and on into the Northwest is physically unlike the two California-bound routings which are also single track. Each one of those lines features several hundred miles of desolate desert roadbed. Providing only a modicum of originating traffic off their seemingly endless, sage-covered wastes, the not-so-forgotten Western Pacific and the old Los Angeles and Salt Lake Railroad trails serve their purpose as connectors. Although the line through Idaho performs a similar function, it adds major traffic in its own right, both for shipments to other states as well as regional activity.

Granger, Wyoming, won't be readily found on a large scale map of the American West, but that in no way diminishes its luster. The name encompasses a few dozen homes, a 40-mph dual-control switch turnout, stoically designated CP 847—one of 1,500 push buttons west of Omaha— along with a 15,057-foot-long siding that allows a dispatcher certain latitude in blending traffic onto the busy double-tracked Green River Division main line.

On a warm summer day, backdropped by a sky of blue azure with cloud decks stacked to a far horizon, Granger offers an initial peek at the northernmost of UP's triangular forks pointed at the Pacific Ocean.

Visible at long range on a wide curve, cast in slow motion by distance, a tiny thread of a silhouette seems to be making its way out of the east. Minutes tick by, eventually confirming that it is after all a train, not an illusion of dancing heat waves.

But which way is it going? Ogden or Pocatello?

Discovery comes soon, for looming large is a multicolored stack train. The doppler effect of its air horn drifts above a grade crossing, and traction motors howl in a swirling cocoon of dust. This one's for Ogden, and probably Salt Lake City. Quickly, it fades away, cabooseless.

Soon, almost in the expected UP fashion of bunched train movements, another far-off ribbon appears above the sea of sagebrush, westbound. Just maybe this fellow's bound for Pocatello. Meanwhile, an eastbound line of boxcars and loaded lumber flats snakes through the junction, occupying space reserved for Salt Lake Division moves. It's doubtful a dispatcher would allow this crossover movement in front of the other oncoming train were it heading for Utah.

Drifting down to 40, the arriving freight proves to be pure piggyback, with Seattle or Portland on its mind. Trailers swaying, it heads through a compensating curve, then straightens out past an extensive cluster of cattle chutes.

While essentially single track over its 214-mile kingdom, the Pocatello Subdivision offers well-placed portions of two-track running that relieve choke points, a feature the railroad displays elsewhere in the Northwest. At Kemmerer, where an important coal and sulphur mine branch takes off south, there are eight miles of twin steel.

Stretching east and west through Montpelier, Idaho, is a 12.5-mile section of double track. Some 25 miles east of Pocatello another double-track segment begins, bringing trains of the Pocatello Sub and the Ogden Sub—which join the line at McCammon, Idaho—into the Pocatello terminal.

A dispatcher sitting back there viewing Omaha's high-tech display knows that if movements are clustering—a normal situation for this railroad—relief is available in several places without missing a beat in the tempo. Trains can be flip-flopped, the fast past the slow, meets of important opposites made so smoothly that none are delayed. This is not always the case, mind you, but without this system the daily march would take a lot longer.

Spreading a topographical map of the United States across a table reveals the diagonal path that the UP's main line takes across Idaho and toward the Northwest. Note how the line approaches the Idaho–Wyoming state line at an oblique angle, determined by a group of mountains that spreads on a north-south axis all the way from mid-Utah to southern Montana. Picking its way through this region while creating as little altitude see-saw as possible involves passing through a series of valleys between Granger and Pocatello. Then once past Pocatello, the wide swinging course of the Snake River is followed by steel on a western vector before making a turn north toward Huntington, Oregon, and the Blue Mountains, avoiding a broad mass of mountaintops extending from Boise all the way through Canada.

Eastern Idaho exhibits a long, slender valley north of Idaho Falls that provided the surveyors with a route into Montana.

The Ogden–Salt Lake City and Pocatello routes beyond Granger form two legs of a regional triangle, the third of which is the Salt Lake City–Pocatello route. This latter ranks as a secondary line, a fact that is easily determined by the lack of representation on the Omaha Bunker's wall panel.

Westward from Granger, physical transition occurs as western Wyoming's sprawling tablelands and plateaus give way to Idaho's vast lava plains. Initially the only identifiable difference on the railroad is the change from the Rawlins Subdivision's double-track to the single-track operations of the Pocatello Sub.

Having spiked its steel into Idaho, UP encounters a subtle geographic change as the land becomes a bit more level, displaying signs of an agricul-

Opposite: A westbound leaves from Granger, Wyoming, the linkup between routes that go to California and those that go to the Northwest. The twin tracks in the foreground lead toward Ogden, Utah.

A
A
BEGIN CTC

tural domain. Approaching McCammon a track is seen coming in from the south—the Salt Lake City connection. Twin sets of rail extend over the next two dozen miles to Pocatello's big retarder yard. This, plus an additional 10 miles of double track west of town, provide a dispatcher with significant flexibility in what would otherwise be a crowded zone. Trains can be cleared out of the yard without holding up an inbound arrival, or the reverse. The strategic utilization of limited stretches like this is a UP trademark, hastening overall system performance.

While Hinkle takes care of the Northwest's classification needs, and North Platte literally serves almost the entire railroad, Pocatello ministers more to regional needs. Humps fan out into a 40-track bowl where 60 to 70 percent of all inbound trains are sorted out before moving on. Principal activity centers around sorting traffic on the east-west flow, while cars going north into Montana and south into Utah and California are represented to a lesser degree.

Pocatello, you may recall, is the stuff of rail lore, immortalized in the ever-famous work ethic as a "Pocatello Night Yardmaster," always good for inclusion in a service letter.

Like UP's main lines everywhere, the rhythm of life at Pocatello is syncopated. Mornings may see a dominant eastbound flow, stack and trailer trains OS'd out of town ahead of less-important symbols, while a westbound container run from an East Coast port is clearing hours before a crowd follows behind it. Meantime, the Butte ore train is keeping out of the way, creeping through a yard track, where, untouched by switchers, it will take on a fresh crew and depart, behind a trio of SD40s.

Through all this, two SD yard goats, snowplows removed, are herding cars over the hump, preceded by a loud siren as the initial cars coast into any number of possible tracks in the bowl below. Freight cars, singly or in groups, are funneled to their proper niche as a computer marks their speed, weighs how many other cars are in each track, then applies just the proper pinch of pressure. Grouped, they're extracted from bowl tracks and formed into mile-long symbols, PCSC (Pocatello–Salt Lake City), PCNPP (Pocatello–North Platte Perishables), or a PCHK (Pocatello–Hinkle), to name but a few.

Where once Union Pacific was renowned for its deluxe stable of streamlined "Cities," *Portland, Los Angeles* and *San Francisco,* today's version of passenger service rests upon a slim offering provided by Amtrak. Not that people in charge mind, for the money's elsewhere and first-class service is a losing proposition. Just notice how many opposing moves, even the hottest, get tagged with siding time as a varnish moves across the district. Handling a small number of people creates a disproportionate concept of favored treatment where freight pays the bills.

One of the Amtrak schedules (there are but three west of Omaha) connects Portland with Salt Lake City. Crossing most of Idaho in darkness, Amtrak's Nos. 25 and 26 are allocated a four-minute stop in Pocatello

In a scene typical of ranch country in southeast Idaho, an SD60M leads a freight toward the next big terminal, Green River.

during the wee hours of the morning. During their passage, many an engine cab will resound to "red over green, goin' siding," as the single set of hard metal ribbons across Idaho's extensive grasslands and farms is normally well stocked with trains.

Southern Idaho is a broad belt of extensive agriculture, given to crops that demand large tracts of land. Pictorially, it is somewhat of a cross between western Nebraska and the Palouse country of Washington–Idaho. Gentle, graceful curvature alternates with miles of soft incline, more likely to drain off a throttle than call for sustained stress. There are no communities of note on the 242-mile-long Nampa Subdivision (Pocatello–Nampa), just a clutch of undistinguished sidings alternating with dusty farm towns. There's just enough interim demand to call locals on duty and to create a through freight to make the necessary pickups and setouts along the route, except in harvest season when two or three hamlets may push out enough carloadings to generate a full-sized movement.

An engineer called for duty naturally asks, "What for?" Preference is shown for an NPSEZ (North Platte–Seattle hotshot), which is a racehorse in comparison to the oft-interrupted endurance run of the PCNA (Pocatello–Nampa). Working a lashup of SD40s or early U-boats through town after town where cars need to be switched is a tiresome but vital ingredient of railroading. Poking 40 to 50 cars of slack into grain elevators or industrial stubs can't compare with the exhilaration of force-feeding energy to a troika of fast-wheeling thoroughbreds with recent builders' tags. Here as elsewhere there is a definite class distinction in a lineup. Only the names are different from anyplace else; otherwise, locomotive performance is displayed equally well in Idaho as it is in Nebraska and Kansas.

More toward the west, Glenns Ferry and Mountain Home, the landscape blends into widespread grassland, dissected by canyons and low-lying hills. Roadbed widens to a 40-mile section of two-track running, creating an opportunity for some artful maneuvering in an area where, on occasion, a single trailing unit can be observed assisting westbounds across mild gradations in cross-section.

Boise, the state's largest city, is served by a 44-mile cut-off, rather than being served by mainline rail. Hinged at either end by whirring power switches, the bypass is an important source of waybills, despite its seemingly off-center site.

Nampa provides a meeting forum for two operating entities, the 927-mile Pocatello Division, which blankets most of Idaho, and the 842-mile Nampa Division, which crosses into Oregon. Centered in a wide agricultural valley, Nampa is a prime originating base for frigid mechanical reefers. In years past, an eastbound perishable movement known as the Nampa Fruit drew first breath here. An archetypical division point, it is long and slender, providing enough local need to keep a switch crew busy, consolidating and blocking cars from several area branch lines which provide a mix of what farm and forest can produce, frequently responding to a seasonal surge.

Tonnage is added to passing freights while others are born here, swelling the daily number that sweep through a natural breach in the landscape near Glenns Ferry or travel the solitude of moonlit fields toward Pocatello and Wyoming.

Idaho is both typical and atypical Union Pacific. The long, thrusting single iron that links the double-tracked high plains highway with northwestern states is all that is expected. Dominated by the latest in motive power design, up-to-the-minute signaling techniques, and periodically surveyed by track geometry cars, its ability is taken for granted. A collection of branch lines, sugar beet harvests, and tracks jammed with mechanical reefers is not.

Like any other major component of Union Pacific, Idaho is its own image—different and the same all at once.

Opposite: Crew change completed, a general freight rolls eastward out of Pocatello, Idaho, on a snowy morning in March 1989.

9162
9162
9147
9147

X-61
X-61
U.P. 61
UNION
PACIFIC

UNIQUE POWER

"THAT MACHINE COULD only belong to Union Pacific!"

There was a time when Union Pacific marched to its own tune. Atypical motive power designs, a willingness to experiment, and individualism pretty much characterized UP motive power development from the early 1950s through the 1970s.

Originally, the now-traditional yellow was applied to standard carbody designs that just about everyone else had received. The blended noses of EMD F units and the blunter sheet metal work of similar offerings from Alco's Schenectady erecting bays differed no bit from similar equipment on the Santa Fe, Southern Pacific, Northern Pacific or a baker's dozen other railroads. Yet until the 3,000-hp SD40 emerged, with its almost total standardization, UP had shown a marked willingness to test a variety of forms on its rails. Over these years of trial and question the western carrier had exhibited several examples of motive power that would never draw so much as a breath anywhere else. To put it succinctly, this was UP's era of unique motive power.

On a major carrier such as UP, motive power classes come and go over time on a routine basis. They are, after all, expendable capital investments calculated to generate so much effort per axle, while toting up ever increasingly monthly mileage stats as technology and improving materials arrive with each generation.

There has been nothing, however, to ever match the turbine age of the 1950s and 1960s. These jet-powered locomotives were an exceptional breed, a one-of-a-kind contribution to railroad lore. In their time it seemed almost logical they would appear, roaming the high plains of Nebraska and the blue sky panorama of Wyoming.

An attempt to match turbine engine design—popularized by its adaptation to airborne commerce—with the requirements of surface hauling would culminate in a combine of silhouette and sound which no other American railroad has ever experienced in routine action. Nor, for that matter, has any other carrier seriously considered this breed beyond experimental glimpses.

Opposite: Among the double-engined units UP purchased on a sampling basis from GE, EMD and Alco, this set of Century 855s from Alco never did very well, and UP ordered no more. In the photo they're seen accelerating east from Ogden, Utah.

Not quite willing to leave diesel locomotive development exclusively to ideas created by outside thinkers, Union Pacific offered a few original ideas of its own following World War II, plus a willingness to back them with a checkbook. The result was a class of outsized haulers whose capacity for work was at least legendary if not especially enduring over the long haul.

On a cold day in winter, one of the last series of huge turbines could work 2,000 tons more up the hill out of Ogden than tonnage ratings called for. In the hot, thin air of summer you deducted from what those numbers called for. Such were the vagaries of jet-powered trains.

Low fuel costs coupled with high horsepower from a turbine prime mover, plus a projected prowess to haul weighty freight trains over lengthy stages at speed, proved to be a genesis for turbine creation. When in 1948 General Electric assembled locomotive frame serial number 30159, and sprayed it with what would become traditional UP yellow, the turbine age was at hand. The railroad provided digital sequence number 50 for the occasion.

This initial locomotive was a total proof-of-concept machine, manufactured to experience a host of tests and trials. Would this or that work, and why or why not?

This was to be the role of roster occupant number 50.

Economics of gas turbine design as applied to mainline usage rested in a source of relatively low-cost fuel. While the turbine burned considerably more fuel than a diesel prime mover, this could be offset by low-cost

Assisted up the hill by a "chicken-wire" F unit, turbine No. 59 comes out of the canyons west of Evanston, Wyoming, and settles down for the long, expansive horizons to be found in western Wyoming.

On a cold morning in November, No. 7 threads the yard switches in Ogden, Utah, its jet blast at low ebb but will be at full throttle when the last car enters the main track.

bunker-type residual oil. The potentially powerful turbine—4,500 hp in an 83-foot-long carbody—compared favorably with a similar amount cast in a three-unit set of 1,500 hp per EMD F7s. There was 375 horsepower per axle on this standard diesel model of its time, while a turbine, if it panned out, offered promise of much greater brawn.

It is interesting to note that today's diesel fleet, dominated by 3,800-hp SD60s and 4,000-hp Dash-8s, provide power-per-axle ratios that only now are coming close to number 50, which for its time represented a quantum advance in drawbar pull.

Successful experiences with turbine number 50 prompted the railroad to order 10 units for heavy freight hauling. Similar in overall look to number 50, they differed modestly in having a single cab, whereas number 50 had been outshopped with a double end. Assigned to territory primarily west of Cheyenne, they were soon racking up monthly mileages in routine fashion, although their demonstrably loud jet-engine exhaust limited their odyssey to the road's more barren rights-of-way.

The initial turbine series displayed numbers 51–60, with the first example entering road service in January 1952, and the last arriving in midsummer 1953. Due to their high fuel flow rates they were—in comparison with diesels—relatively short-legged. Ultimately, their range was extended by adding a separate fuel tender, a measure then adapted for the next two classes of jet-powered locomotives to come along. As to comparisons with steam engines, UP's famous 4-8-8-4 *Big Boys* were rated at 130,000 pounds of drawbar pull at eight mph, while the turbine created 150,000 pounds at a similar pace.

After number 60's arrival completed the first order, UP opted for a second class, numbers 61–75. While basically similar in internal performance, their outward appearance differed by having an open porch down each side. Eventually the railroad had home-converted 24,000-gallon tenders tacked on, augmenting an on-board fuel capacity. The few hundred SD40s which would eventually saturate UP's 1980s roster carry a 4,000-gallon tank, while the latest high-horsepower units with their long-range potential hold 5,000 gallons. The difference in fuel needs between turbine and diesel are thus obvious.

By 1956 there were 25 turbines working the line between Cheyenne and Ogden, performing mostly at an altitude of 5,000–6,000 feet in summer's heat and winter's frosty breath. With the full complement of these "little turbines," UP credited 12 percent of the system's total ton miles to them. Racking up an average of 100,000 productive miles a year, the turbine's future seemed assured.

With Union Pacific, like other roads being clenched in a competitive vise between the necessity of running heavier trains for cost reasons and faster trains for need, a solution of even more powerful axial flow engines seemed reasonable.

Between mid-1958 and mid-1961 General Electric was again engaged to bring forth what would be the ultimate brand of gas-turbine locomotive. Numbered 1 through 30, these 8,500-hp behemoths measured about 179 feet in a three-unit arrangement, tipping the scale at 598 tons. The actual turbine was carried in the second unit, while the first housed a control compartment, plus an auxiliary diesel engine for hostling, since turbine operating characteristics were most economical at full output. In fact, while idling, a turbine burned close to 40 percent of its maximum fuel flow when hauling tonnage. The third unit was a tender.

The birth of these more potent turbine units had some rough moments in design, arriving a year later than expected. But they, too, were to figure prominently in calculations of annual freight tonnage. Massive in look, brutish in ability, they could walk a heavy train up the 1.14 percent grade of the canyon east of Ogden at a steady 17 mph. In later years, even this performance was deemed inadequate, and several turbines were configured to ride tandem with diesel prototypes. As originally created, the large turbines were rated at 8,500 hp. With experience under its belt the railroad subsequently upgraded their ability to 10,000 hp, surely the largest such equation yet to appear in a singular measure of internal combustion motive power proficiencies.

During September 1960, UP had 19 of the newer, heavier turbines posted to its western lines' call-boards. Average monthly mileage figures were 11,776, with 12.6 percent of system gross ton-miles being generated by them. That same month 75 spanking-new SD24s and 30 new GP20 diesel-electrics in comparable duty stations over the same territory averaged 12,110 and 12,322 miles per unit, respectively. So the turbines were doing a very creditable job.

The SD24 introduced the basic C-C type truck to the road, a style that in later years would and still does dominate its choice for footwear.

Eventually several things conspired to shorten the operating career of the turbine fleet. Their life span was shorter than diesel-electrics, perhaps because of maintenance issues. Though touted as being comparatively simple compared to a more commonplace unit from EMD, their small numbers made them exceptional, calling for special servicing and handling. This is never a favorable position among those who must keep a roster running. Go to a predominantly EMD road and ask about minority GE units and you'll find that most people favor the former. Reverse these roles, so will the answers.

By 1963 the early 51-class engines had all been turned back to General Electric, where their span-bolster underframes would be refurbished to continue life as underpinnings of yet another unusual UP idea, the twin-motored U50s.

In practice, turbine blades, so elemental a component of this form of power, were to prove a weakness. They required replacement more often than calculated, while the shock and stress of train movements would turn up problems which rarely if ever afflicted stationary turbine installations upon which performance had been predicted.

Perhaps the most damaging blow to the turbines' continued presence was the most elemental premise, low fuel prices, which would offset its ravenous appetite—when compared with a diesel. Time had found alternate uses for the residual fuel which was a turbine's life line. So as prices for this energy source rose, the turbine's impact on UP's roster diminished. By the early 1970s "turbine power" was a topic for historians to mull over, success or lack of it merely a debate topic.

Actually, numbers 1–30 had fallen from grace years before, their final depreciation taken for granted by another series of Union Pacific locomotives, which again were to prove totally unlike anything else rolling through the yards and junctions of America.

In retrospect, the turbine's existence on Union Pacific might be compared to Southern Pacific's experience with the European diesel-hydraulic locomotive. Each potentially had something going for it: lower cost operations or superior performance to the then production-line diesel-electric of stock size and talent. Both represented a gamble, an alternative approach to ongoing lines of development then in vogue. Neither was to survive for the normal duration of a conventional diesel unit, since the promissory note created was never fully stamped "paid."

The Double Ones

Individualism for Union Pacific motive power—as exemplified by its stable of turbines—was not to be the only course in a railroad world more noted for conformity than not. With UP's extensive geographic spread and needs it seemed that a bit of customizing in locomotive design could pay off to a degree not seen elsewhere. At least it was worth an attempt. For indeed the turbines had offered that potential if perhaps a bit radically on a modest scale.

Basically, the Omaha-based line had entered the diesel age just like anyone else, bringing aboard F units, Alco FAs and ultimately Geeps as they evolved during this first generation of a new motive power age. Like

One of UP's double ones, a U50, idles outside the shops at Cheyenne, Wyoming.

Looking something like a designer's nightmare, the one and only trio of Alco Century 855s comes across the Green River Bridge with a reefer train.

so many other railroads, the bulk of orders clearly favored La Grange-built products. Perhaps unusual were the GP cabless B units followed by similar thinking when the low-nosed SD24s appeared, but overall, armour yellow came along in rather traditional form in the numbers necessary to power a large western carrier.

Yet for a railroad that brought out such graceful examples of steam engines as the svelte 800-class 4-8-4s and the now world-famous *Big Boys,* the contemporary diesel crop seemed a bit wanting.

From this belief stemmed another dimension of UP dieseldom that no other railroad has ever had—with one minor exception—the twin-motored era. It is true that Espee did take a sampling of such units, a trio each from builders GE and EMD, but more as an exploratory look-see than anything else. UP was the unquestioned champion of twin-motored freight power during the 1960s and 1970s.

Just why?

The answer lies in the railroad's operating style and environment described previously: long trains, fast trains, plus a huge expanse of the nation with a less than easygoing profile in which to match competition both off and on rails.

Enter a massive-appearing heavyweight out of General Electric's Erie manufacturing base, the flat-faced U50. Electro-Motive provided their version of what UP might come to admire in a twin and labeled it DD35. Not to be outdone, though, in the final stages of their quest to stay afloat, the engineering stylists at Alco came up with an absolutely huge abstraction termed the Century 855, and sent it west for consideration. While many GE and EMD twin-engined products soon joined UP's roster, the trio of 855s turned out to be an unsuccessful stepchild.

The time of the twin-motored titans had arrived. It would span about two dozen annual reports.

Unlike the turbines, whose roamings were a bit restricted by their loud

During the 1960s, the UP was given over to buying large units and assigning them low numbers. Here we see UP's second DD35A leading a westward manifest through Evanston, Wyoming.

singing, and their special needs for fuel, the big twins were essentially oversized units that gulped standard diesel fuel available anywhere.

In some circles the twins were simply two Geeps in one.

It is not just enough to purchase a high horsepower locomotive unit. The initial cost is only one measure to contemplate; of at least equal impact is the unit's fuel bill and maintenance needs. A design that offers early assurances of performance may prove to be a costly dependent in later life. The rap on the twins was that when one was down for routine service or maintenance, in effect, two units were off line. It only took a problem with one engine to shut down the entire unit. People who are responsible for moving trains have a problem with that.

It would seem appropriate that the final example of UP's immense twin units would prove to be its most spectacular. Superlatives abound in describing the 6,600-hp DDA40X of 1969–1971 delivery dates.

Union Pacific has always had—at least in the diesel era—what could be titled a *Number One* class of engine, meaning the latest and most powerful units. Assigned to priority trains with their gearing good for 80 mph, the 6900 class DDA40Xs belied their 545,000-pound mass as they raced to and fro across mountain, plain and desert alike, pitting their 6,600 hp against the time clock's impatient demands. Like the turbines before it, and the ubiquitous SD40s and Dash-8s to come, the DDA40X was to be a center of attention in its time.

Fancy now how two of them might have looked in years past. Hitched to a low-tonnage but high-class piggyback schedule out of Los Angeles they would take the measure of Cajon Pass, and storm across the high desert to tackle Cima Hill amid a dwarf's forest of Joshua trees. Not too many hours later, Meadow Valley Wash north of Las Vegas would be sounding to their dogged persistence. Quickly, Salt Lake City would be just another memory as flanges squealed along the climbing curves pointed at Wyoming. Over the border at Wasatch and downhill they'd flow, their throttles intermittently in run-eight on the plateaus into Green River. Soon, though, it would be North Platte's giant yard scheme and the free-flowing Nebraska subs to either flank. In these assignments and over the widely separated towns they would age in a hurry.

Officially, the 6900's vitals were listed as, weight, 545,000 pounds; length, 98 feet, five inches; power, two 16-645E3A engines throwing out 6,600 hp and current to eight traction motors. Carrying 8,200 gallons of fuel and dubbed the *Centennial,* this team of 46 members was destined to marshal high-speed trains on the UP during the 1970s.

Already, though, even as the *Centennials* were performing their stellar roles, important rethinking was taking root. For a railroad whose mechanical department had been so original in developing turbines, double-motored locomotives, and mainline B-units during the second generation, Union Pacific did a complete about face with the advent of EMD's SD40, 3,000-hp model.

Gone were the days when customized models had been the forte. Now standardization took over with a vengeance. It had actually started even before the DDA40X had arrived on the scene. The initial SD40 order was in 1966; the last in 1980, with an update to the SD40-2 modification taking place in 1972. This represents a 15-year period during which the SD40 came to rule the order books almost to the exclusion of anything else in the C-C bracket of wheel arrangement. The exception involved General Electric's U30C during the early 1970s, and later its evolutionary follow-on, the C30-7, toward the end of that decade.

This is by no means any attempt to detail UP's roster, because it includes many B-B trucked units, and a few odds and ends such as a half-dozen GP40Xs with a 1978 builder's date. The bulk of units employed in mainline, heavy-duty service ride on three-axle trucks. The "Forties" came to be the domineering diesel type in that business.

Other western railroads came to rely more upon the 3,600-hp SD45, especially Southern Pacific. UP did have an early class of this model, numbered 1–50. Originally classified into the 3600 series upon its advent in 1965, it never caught on in UP's west. Consequently, the 3,000-hp SD40 flooded terminal service tracks in later years.

This almost complete conversion to a type of locomotive that employs a single prime mover based upon the EMD 16-645E3 motor, is as typical of the railroad as its earlier dedication to the unconventional. If standardization was to prevail, then so be it—by the hundreds.

Starting with the number 3000—rather appropriate based upon size—SD40s were added till they reached into the upper 3900 series, though not always consecutively. By late 1989 the last SD40-2 bore the number 4321 on its cab sides, bolstered by inclusion of MoPac engines into the sequence.

Yet even here there would be variants. From 1973 to 1979 four separate orders of SD40-2s were placed in the 8000–8099 series. Like the huge

Produced to coincide with the 100th anniversary of the completion of the trans-continental railroad in 1869, UP 6900 class was *the* prime mover on the road's more important trains for many a year. With the demise of this series of locomotives, UP pretty much ended its role as an innovator of motive power design. The locale is the foot of Cajon Pass.

Centennials, they were designed for speed, bringing 80-mph gearing in the form of a 59/18 ratio, even as the more commonplace SD40s were coming aboard with 62/15 gear ratio, calculated for a 65-mph top pace.

In later years, the 8000s would be regeared, dropping their maximum performance level back to that of the bulk of such units. They were also renumbered into the 3000–4000 block as well. However, every once in a while, even in 1989, a faded paint job reveals a barely discernible "8000," a holdover from when these engines were the fastest freight power UP owned outside the big double Geeps or *Centennials.*

Today all the principal UP C-C locomotive classes are allowed a 70-mph maximum speed.

Union Pacific's motive power individuality seemed to have died when the last DDA40X was uncoupled and shuffled off into storage. In a way, the huge installment buying of several hundred SD40s and their derivatives, the Dash-2s, represented a capitulation to concepts of mass production this railroad had grudgingly resisted for years.

The turbines, the U50s, DD35s and the massive but elegant DDA40Xs were a statement. "While we can't ignore benefits of standardization collectively, our railroad is just a bit different and with our special needs there's always room for a class of motive power to suit."

Now those days appear to be gone.

On the other hand, UP still seems to be following its own path. Notice how on other western railroads the three-axled, six-motored unit appears

Not for sharp radius curves . . . a pair of DDA40Xs starts the downward run through Cajon Pass on what has become a typically smoggy day in that locale.

to be falling from grace. Southern Pacific and Santa Fe have opted for large buys of powerful B-B units. UP's taste, however, still rides on the C-C truck locomotive, basically two new styles, one each from GE and EMD.

Given the large number of such units purchased in recent years, the yellow fleet represents the youngest average age of any major railroad in the West.

So why does Union Pacific buck conventional wisdom in relying upon six-axled engines when trends indicate the B-B style is favored? Each style has its pluses and minuses, but two-axled trucks tend to wander slightly more on tangent rail than do longer designs. Three-axled trucks tend to generate less wear on straightaways, and more scuffing on curves. So, state your preference and write a check.

X-61
UNION
PACIFIC
981.26

Opposite: Twin prime movers chortling as only an Alco could, the lone trio of Century 855 units strains on the upgrade of Weber Canyon on a warm summer day in Utah.

In the sixties and seventies, Union Pacific had a rather unusual appetite for double motors, a fad that never seemed to catch on at any other U.S. railroad. Here, a couple of DD35s power a freight through Weber Canyon in northern Utah.

The blunt, massive nose section of a DDA40X waits silently on a siding at the top of Cajon Pass, its engines muted after it had been set out because of wheel problems.

STOWE HARDWARE
STOP
UNION PACIFIC
UNION PACIFIC
2436
2436
2436

The SD45 never really caught on with Union Pacific. Its first few came in the 3600 series, but those numbers were eventually vacated to make way for the hundreds of SD40s which eventually became the railroad's standard prime mover.

Opposite: Rolling between industrial buildings near downtown Kansas City, C30-7 No. 2436, and SD40-2 No. 4154, an ex-MoPac unit, lead an eastbound off the UP and onto MoPac rails in the terminal area.

Not part of a numerically large roster class, GP40X No. 93 rumbles through Huntington, Oregon, on the point of one of UP's company specials.

LMS . . . Controlling All That Power

In today's atmosphere you don't run locomotives, you manage them as the multimillion-dollar investments they are. The MKT-UP-MoPac roster of August 1, 1989, lists 2,940 units of diesel power. In terms of replacement value the cost would hover around three billion dollars. Perhaps 55–60 percent of those units would be earning their keep on the original UP system at any moment—or they should if the recently installed computer system to manage locomotive assignments works as expected.

Four times on a 24-hour clock, at 6 A.M., noon, 6 P.M. and midnight, a healthy sized IBM computer in Omaha stops whatever instructions it might be working on to devote the next hour or so on wide-ranging contingencies, like what is the best assignment for one and all of the nearly 3,000 diesel locomotives on hand. On file is an itemized history of every engine, its systemwide capabilities and whether shopping or inspections are needed.

The Locomotive Management System, or LMS, is a complex software program which speeds through a huge volume of calculations to command locomotive assignments—from Chicago to Seattle, from Dallas to Los Angeles, even on a remote branch line in northern Idaho. It's all there to be updated every few hours.

LMS's stated primary goal is neither to reduce costs nor increase locomotive fleet utilization, but to provide just enough power to run all trains, to provide it on time, and to "match" the best set of units for each type of train. An organizational arrangement has established locomotive managers across the system with fourfold responsibilities: a) provide locomotives for today's trains; b) plan power assignments for future trains; c) analyze equipment requirements, cost and reliability for all trains; and d) route maintenance-due units to the proper shop at the right moment.

Since diesels can be routed across the entire system at will, the complexity involved is massive, and consequently, is fundamentally only resolvable by computer. Consider this daily, ongoing puzzle for up to 700 potential trains. How many trains will actually run today, how many in the next few days? What train will run where, what units are available for them and what is the expected tonnage involved? Will it be a time-sensitive "Z" train or a drag?

Power balancing needs must be assessed as well; outbound and inbound locomotive movements across dozens of subdivisions have to be scanned so that arriving engines of the proper stature can be hitched to outbound trains without delay.

Other parameters considered include how a locomotive will perform over varied geographical territory and with different types of trains. A particular model might do better with stack trains, and less well when coupled to a unit grain train. The current assignment of SD60s to the bulk

Mainline action near Cheyenne, Wyoming, as a piggyback train hurries west with a five-unit set of SD40-2s, including MKT No. 611, while in the opposite heading another one moves on toward Nebraska.

With the addition of so many road units the last three years and the existence of so many SD40s already on the roster, UP has downgraded many 3,000-hp units to yard switcher status as demonstrated by No. 3958 at Green River in August 1990.

of UP's coal moves illustrates that point along with the transfer of SD50s to chemical train service on MoPac's south lines.

Linking locomotive management with train management means that Omaha's "Bunker" plays its part, too. The all-seeing eye there feeds real time enlightenment to LMS. Best characterized as a railroad's version of a computer dating service, LMS matches the personality of trains with the traits of almost 3,000 diesel locomotives. When you own that much motive power, computer-supported decision making becomes a necessity.

The "Bunker" knows that a grain train has fallen off projections because of traffic density at Hilgard's 9,295-foot-long siding in the Blue Mountains; it knows what units are primed and waiting on the outbound tracks at North Platte's busy terminal. It comprehends these things in milliseconds, shares it secrets with LMS, which in turn ponders them in almost unfathomable terms, and ultimately explains that the best way to run a railroad at midday is. . . ! Six hours later, as the human masters are enjoying a cup of coffee, the computer may change its mind. It does this often, in a most comprehensive manner.

As each train's performance is logged, the computer projects operating demands for the coming seven days. Minute by minute, hour by hour, data is punched in over the company's information network. The traffic control center at the Harriman Dispatch Center, locomotive manning needs, plus the company's National Car System Control Center in St. Louis contribute to that torrent. As rolling stock is moved, cars interchanged, or empty cars simply parked on a stub track somewhere, the systemwide equation is subtly altered.

A half-dozen empty well cars may have to be in Oakland two days from now; perhaps a lumber mill requires an extra wood chip car on the Idaho Northern Branch tomorrow. And there's always the U.S. Army. A pair of unit trains is needed next month to run from Ft. Riley, Kansas, to Ft. Irwin, California. Those M-1 tanks and armored personnel carriers will soak up a lot of trailer train flats with their sometimes mile-and-a-half-long extensions. Better start thinking about where they'll come from, as well as what units will propel them.

As to more arcane matters, LMS states how each diesel unit is equipped, exactly how much and when maintenance is required and just what shop will be available. On a more personal note it totes up running repair stats for each model on the roster, which includes fuel efficiency plus actual running repair costs. Foreign road units are also told where they need to be returned.

Oh yes, if a diesel is now working in some consist, LMS reckons when it will be available for its next assignment.

When the appointed hour arrives, Omaha's computer considers the LMS program by simulating the next seven days' railroading; it chooses an arbitrary set of units from its data base, assigns them to run expected trains and then calculates the cost, while taking into account the latest tidings from Harriman's TCS. With this as a foundation it processes all combinations of motive power for all trains, a six-billion-plus set of variables, involving 23 billion computer instructions. The IBM mainframe can handle 74 million instructions per second, in case you wondered.

That six-hour update tells which combination allows the most trains to be run at the least cost.

Welcome to the contemporary world of big league railroading where absolutely nothing is traditional nor sacrosant.

Having identified the need, the computer's final step is to assign specific locomotives to actual trains. Not too much, never too little is the credo. Ultimately, it becomes a "consist builder," satisfying the horsepower flow over the next 24 hours by matching Dash-8s, SD40s or 60s to their symbols. Nor are locals or specials ignored. They too have been recognized by the great numbers-cruncher.

This mighty flow of electrons bearing instructions is forwarded to the "Bunker," where flashing lights portray decisions one step further along in the scheme.

This is how No. 6189 came to be working a 110-car string of coal empties along the North Platte Sub to South Morrill, or how a C36-7 sat around Rupert, Idaho, overnight, idling away the hours before tomorrow's dawn, when it whistled out of town with a set of noisy mechanical reefers. The computer did it!

Portland, Oregon's Albina Yard finds a local train and its caboose heading down the ladder track to pick up a train.

UP's latest and largest horsepower units from GE and EMD combine to move a solid reefer train eastward up the slopes of Sherman Hill in the summer of 1988.

The New Breed—UP's Super Engines

Dash-8s, SD60s. . . . These are the first-class engines of today's mainline thinking, and Union Pacific refers to them as its "Super Engines." Not only in the sense of horsepower, but because they represent the latest electronic technology, the black box era.

It is somewhat curious how Union Pacific refers to its current generation of powerful locomotives, curious because in past decades the railroad actually had larger, more beefy engines cast in armour yellow than it does presently. The turbines, the huge double-motored behemoths of the '50s, '60s and '70s have yet to be equaled in single hoods by today's designers. Then as SD40s became standard fare on trains beyond Omaha, they came to represent, at least singly, less than the 3,600-hp standard to which other western railroads were adhering. So while the 4,000-hp Dash-8 and 3,800-hp SD60s represent a quantum leap over several hundred basic SD40s, and follow-on Dash-2 variants, they really aren't that much more powerful in pure tonnage ratings than the SD45s and U36Cs to which other carriers had grown accustomed.

In fact, the appellation "super" has its meaning far beyond a singular muscular contour, as it stands for the latest in technology—such as onboard computers, ease of maintenance, and reliability in train service—ideas which have been expressed in other industries for quite some time. It also represents a minor gamble, for the railroad operates in a harsh environment. The continual shock and strain of hauling heavyweight movements at high speed, or over hilltops, is something few other machines are challenged to accomplish for months and years on end. Five or six years will effectively determine whether today's black boxes are equal to the medals they have already been awarded.

Meantime, a brief glimpse of today's livery.

As referred to earlier, the ubiquitous SD40 and subsequent brothers occupied the bulk of this railroad's order book over a 15-year span. So, well into the 1990s, perhaps beyond, this particular EMD model will be forging couplers with everyday trains. To a lesser extent, in terms of roster numbers, so will many of the later U-Boats. Their role will probably be a secondary one, relegated to a less than prime time performance due to age.

Between second-generation power, so liberally ordered throughout the 1970s and today's third generation of power, UP opted for two classes of what has turned out to be interim power: EMD's 3,600-hp SD50 and General Electric's burly C36-7 with 3,750 hp. The latter came to the system by way of Missouri Pacific lettering. The SD50s went to chemical train service in the Southwest, not having panned out well in western territories, being labeled in some circles as a "Band-aid" response to the C36-7. In both instances, the two classes of interim power did not become dominant factors on today's UP roster. Those honors are held by the Dash-8 and SD60, the "high stepper" and the "coal engine," based upon typical assignments. Not that either design will not be found elsewhere, but their early years have been focused upon those specific skills.

GE's squarish-looking Dash-8 40C is well on its way to becoming the most numerous modern diesel on hand. It still has a long way to go to supplant the several hundred SD40s, but as older examples of that type are retired the Dash-8 will undoubtedly predominate, unless of course a newer example rolls from the erecting shop to counter present trends.

Starting with the number 9100 in 1987, the Dash-8 series had reached consecutively up to 9455 by late 1990. By mid-1990 the earliest examples will be ready for a rebuild, given that they turn out five-figure mileage statistics monthly in high-speed train service.

Delivery of the conventional low-nose SD60 began in 1986 with the 6000 and ran through the 6084 by late 1987. Beginning with No. 6085 in 1988 the SD60M, with its wide "North American" cab, was added to the roster and by late 1990 it had reached No. 6268, as these new-look diesels came along in increasing numbers.

The purpose of General Electric's Dash-8 40C is to be routinely more of a speed merchant than the SD60, although both are equally capable of a maximum 70-mph gait. Across the Great Plains, desert corridors and other western assignments, the angular GEs strut their stuff on high steppers to the expected degree for which they were acquired. The manufacturer offers a range of 367,000 to 420,000 pounds for this C-C heavyweight, but UP equips theirs to scale in at 391,000 pounds. Length is 70 feet, eight inches, with the hood encompassing a 16-cylinder GE FDL16 prime mover. Singly or in multiples, the unit can negotiate minimum track curvature of 21 degrees or a 272-foot radius. Gearing is an 83/20 ratio providing a starting tractive effort of 97,750 pounds, with a rating of 77,000 at 1,050 amps on the meter. Its lowest continuous rating is at 11 mph, a circumstance not presumed to be widespread given the normal train assignments offered to the Dash-8s.

What differentiates these latest diesels from their predecessors is the electronic age. Just as computers have absorbed the routine of car counts and dispatching, so has the power unit come to be influenced by technology of this sort. Aboard a Dash-8 an engineer monitors—actually stares at—GE's DID (Diagnostic Display panel). In the arcane world of technologists, it is described as a fast and obviously accurate means of communication between the locomotive handler and computers.

The initial assumption is that a computer functions faster and with more precision than an engineer, yet so-called artificial intelligence is not part of today's units. Simply put, computerized data on performance and statistical summaries don't come with their own decision-making abilities, except for that programmed by humans. Man has not yet been removed from the loop.

Actually, quite a few engineers dispute today's black box mentality, not so much in terms of processing capabilities but in the ideas that have been programmed into them. For instance, there's an engineer running

Just in with a set of coal empties from Kansas City, a 1989-delivered duo of SD60Ms is heading for the service tracks at North Platte before their next assignment.

Oregon's Blue Mountains who gets a queasy feeling every time he heads out of a siding down the 2.2 percent grade. Seems the on-board computer doesn't recognize a brake application for several seconds under certain conditions. Meanwhile, he's through the siding and the power's on for some distance before brake shoes clamp on turning wheels. Although an emergency application can override everything immediately, the slight delay in braking leads to some apprehension based on what lies ahead. For as the hogger says, "An SD40 doesn't behave that way," an attitude displaying fondness for an earlier breed.

Or imagine you're controlling a trio of Dash-8s leading a hotshot across Southern California's Mojave Desert. As the lead engine tops a slight rise you ease back on the throttle. Yet for a few seconds full power continues on all three units, the last two still on the upside, the computer deciding it isn't quite time to relax their effort. It will a few seconds later, but that will take getting used to, especially for those who are individualists.

Welcome to programmed engine handling and the super locomotives.

Besides telling you how to manage your motive power, the computer explains engine faults in green cast language across a flat display screen. Each unit's health is detailed continuously and most faults, however minor, are logged so that terminal inspectors can check them later on. Meanwhile, any restrictions on operating ability are relayed to an engineer and automatically imposed per previous software commands.

In perusing UP's current locomotive ownership there is a single example which displays a greater tractive effort at 1,050 amps of current than it does at starting. That's EMD's SD60, the other member of the super engine stable. Initially, tables show an SD60 capable of overcoming inertia with 98,500 pounds off the starting blocks, but at speeds in the neighborhood of 10 mph, it is rated at 100,000 pounds tractive effort, quite a contrast with most prime movers. The typical diesel falls off 10–15 percent in that speed range, and even more as momentum increases. It is this ability which makes the SD60 a coal business favorite, and under localized conditions on the North Platte Subdivision a solo unit often handles 11,000– 14,000-ton unit trains.

The Next Generation?

Asking about future trends in motive power development is always an exercise in coin flipping, though certain ideas appear to be more logical than others.

The days of a little bit of this and a little bit of that in locomotive units are basically history. Today's motto fits a mold of standardization with flexibility, in some ways a return to the days of the old "F" unit, which was touted as being all things on a railroad.

Present Union Pacific thinking visualizes the roster in three broad categories, beginning with the top-of-the-line "super engines," the highest horsepower units now exemplified by Dash-8s and SD60s. Intermediate diesels in this scheme are today's 3,000–3,300-hp examples, many of which will be running off the miles for years to come considering that SD40s were manufactured to armour yellow specs for 15 years. The third category will be looked upon as light engines, probably in the 2,000–2,250 range, which doesn't necessarily suggest they will be elderly hangovers with a legacy of multiple backshoppings on their record. Many will probably be new since the very high horsepower steeds won't be economically suitable for branchline work, just as articulated steam engines never served as switchers.

Unlike now, when many high-mileage SD40s are seen clattering over retarder yard switches or in branchline duty, the worn-out diesels of tomorrow may simply prove too large and uneconomical for downgrading.

Union Pacific's super engines perform at higher speeds, work harder and pile on miles faster than previous generations of power. Ultimately their life span may prove shorter, not in effort but years. Already the earliest General Electric 4,000-hp models are coming due for major maintenance as the railroad stresses ease of servicing and reliability in design, for with fewer units per train each unit has a more significant burden to bear.

Prior to acquiring the MoPac and the Katy the motive power goal was to slim down to no more than five roster classes, a program postponed temporarily by these events. That standard is still the ultimate, and if all goes as proposed UP management would like to keep the diesel fleet's average age at around seven or eight years.

A general consensus among UP's motive power people is that until now development has been concentrated above the frame, principally in horsepower equivalents. That's not meant to be critical, just factual, and the feeling is that the upper limits of that evolution are being approached, perhaps around 4,500 hp for a solo prime mover with present knowledge. Their belief is that future benefits may unfold from focusing upon traction motor design as an alternative, particularly AC motors. The contemporary DC traction motor has about reached its maximum theoretical capacity, according to this view.

In a less technical but more efficient mode, tomorrow's locomotive is projected to become a mobile administrative office, a trend already well established now that conductors are riding the head end on cabooseless trains. The visionary thinking in Omaha contemplates every major diesel unit being tied directly to the Harriman Dispatching Center and the National Car Distribution Center with its own coordinated cab signals, TV monitor, engine performance monitors and, very probably, a fax machine.

Now that truly is unique!

Illustrating its muscle, a single SD60M works an empty unit coal train on the North Platte Subdivision. Even more muscle will be evident when the same single unit returns over the same territory with a 10,000-plus-ton loaded one.

The latest in Union Pacific's stable of units, a wide-nosed GE C40-8 heads a coal train coming off the Utah Division's Provo Subdivision through Lynndyl, Utah.

3329 3329

EPILOGUE

STEP BACK FOR A MOMENT, contemplate Union Pacific from a distance, both literally and figuratively. You'll discern a railroad that has been and is going places for decades, one of America's earliest and one of today's survivors. Even during Depression days, UP managed to keep going in top shape and entered World War II, not as a capital-starved streak of rust, but as a capable carrier positioned to handle the extra burdens of that period.

Decades of habit long ago transformed themselves into railroading's traditions. Now there are new customs, ones founded upon change itself.

Can you imagine what one of those grizzled veterans of link-and-pin days would think of the here and now? You know, one of those tobacco-chewing, leathery-faced characters minus two fingers . . . the epitome of history's railroad man.

Thousands of miles' worth of choreography visualized and monitored from a single room. Roadside artifacts that read height, width, and sniff out hot journals in milliseconds. Multi-channel linkages aboard locomotives that are capable of diagnosing their own faults via computer and presenting that analysis at shop time. Or for that matter, reams of information about content that not only accompany each train but are projected hundreds of miles away so that this morning's departure from Los Angeles' East Yard will already be scheduled over the hump at North Platte in two days' time, each car precisely in proper sequence and already logged onto the system before the last axle has cleared the yard limit sign in Southern California.

Just imagine yesterday's op attempting to hand off train orders to a few thousand feet of high-flying well cars bearing down at 70 miles per, those by now commonplace versions of modern pinball machines that bounce back and forth on continental jaunts on habitually tight schedules unknown even a few years back.

No longer coupled solely to one-dimensional progress at the drawbar level, railroading today embraces an assortment of technologies.

For a demonstration, contact the Union Pacific Railroad.

Opposite: Having just cut-up an arriving train on one of North Platte's two humps, a switcher climbs back through the retarders for more.

Originating at Hanna and heading east, a unit coal train still has Sherman Hill to conquer and no single unit can handle that task, so a trio of coal engines, the SD60Ms, are working through Rock River on a beautiful summer day.

A short container train attacks Sherman Hill with a pair of 3,000-hp units. The locale is Hermosa on the Laramie side of the mountain.

The statement that UP's steel turnpike never rests is nowhere better illustrated than in Green River. In addition to the several dozen trains rolling through every day, a fair amount of power is also serviced on a continuing basis, as seen here.

Ever-busy Sherman Hill provides many scenes like this, where a westbound shuffles by a load of empty gons still on the climb near Hermosa Siding.

In this winter scene, the westbound steel coil train, possibly the long-distance champion of regular unit trains in America, approaches Portola. This unit train runs from the East Coast to a mill near Pittsburg, California, courtesy of the UP, of course.

Left-hand running's the thing as a freight drops down through the Weber Canyon region on the Utah-Wyoming border.

Opposite: The computer that assigns motive power has a cardinal rule, "Do not overpower," and so a pair of 3,000-hp units is adequate to haul this coal train in the territory around Green River on a westerly jaunt.

3734
3734
UNION PACIFIC
3685

One each of the latest wide cab models offered by GE and EMD rolls along the Utah Division at Moapa, a siding north of Las Vegas.

A westbound exits the final rock-bounded flanks of the Meadow Valley Wash near Farrier Siding.

Struggling up the hill between Kelso and Cima, a freight loaded down with general merchandise is assigned a trio of veteran SD40s.

As seen from the cab, an LACSZ is climbing through Cajon Pass on a December morning.

APL
2400
2400

Opposite: By getting to Oakland, Union Pacific has added a great deal of container traffic to its burgeoning land bridge business. This train originated in the port city and is now approaching Williams Loop.

Along the fringes of the Great Salt Lake, a set of SD40s is assigned to a ballast train. The railroad was forced to raise the roadbed in recent years as the lake waters rose to a historic high.

Two railroads cooperate to run more than a hundred miles of double-track operation across northern Nevada. This UP movement is heading east on its own roadbed, while across the way is SP steel which both roads utilize for their westbound traffic.

No longer does UP use much run-through power, as its recent acquisition of new diesels has canceled the need. On this summer day in 1988, however, a Rio Grande unit was working in partnership with armour yellow units near Nordeen in the Blue Mountains.

A mid-train helper assists a heavy train on its westbound course beyond Huntington, Oregon.

Opposite: More concerned with steady progress than speed, a westbound grain movement moves through one of the many canyons that flank Huntington, Oregon.

3657
3657
UP 3657
UNION
PACIFIC
3757

UNION PACIFIC
3030
UNION PACIFIC
303

UNION PACIFIC
655
UNION PACIFIC
2042
RAILROAD
CROSSING

Opposite, above: Since replaced, this combo was working the retarder yard in Pocatello during the winter of 1988–1989.

Opposite, below: Small units typically run on a UP branch line, in this instance the Idaho Northern branch at Cascade, Idaho.

A local based at Sandpoint pauses at Bonners Ferry, Idaho, to wait for the daily through freight off a Canadian Pacific connection at Eastport before moving on to switch one of the many lumber mills in the state's panhandle.